THERE IS
NO GOD

AND HE IS
ALWAYS WITH YOU

ALSO BY BRAD WARNER

Hardcore Zen

Sex, Sin, and Zen

Sit Down and Shut Up

Zen Wrapped in Karma Dipped in Chocolate

THERE IS
NO GOD

AND HE IS
ALWAYS WITH YOU

A Search for God in Odd Places

Brad Warner

New World Library
Novato, California

New World Library
14 Pamaron Way
Novato, California 94949

Text design by Tona Pearce Myers

Library of Congress Cataloging-in-Publication Data is available.

First printing, June 2013
ISBN 978-1-60868-183-9
Printed in Canada on 100% postconsumer-waste recycled paper

 New World Library is proud to be a Gold Certified Environmentally
Responsible Publisher. Publisher certification awarded by Green Press
Initiative. www.greenpressinitiative.org

10 9 8 7 6 5 4 3 2 1

CONTENTS

Introduction: The Supreme Truth   vii

1. Death in the Holy City   1
2. There Is No God   8
3. ...And He Is Always with You   17
4. Seeing God the Quick, Easy, and Effective Way!   27
5. My Meeting with God, or Enlightenment Porn   34
6. Talking to Zen Monks about God   46
7. Why Call It Buddhism?   57
8. Meditation Is the Practice of Death   64
9. The Meaning of Life   76
10. In Which I Discover the True Meaning of Faith by Going to Finland   83
11. Is Buddha God?   93
12. Sam Harris Believes in God   103
13. Morality and Karma   110
14. Does God Work Miracles in Brooklyn?   120

15. God Doesn't Have to Be Real to Exist   130

16. Suicide at a Zen Monastery   139

17. A Buddhist Christmas in Mexico   145

18. God Holds His Own Hand   153

19. Northern Ireland and the Buddhist Concept of God   159

20. Hotline to Heaven   166

21. What God Wants from You   174

22. God Is Silence   185

About the Author   189

THE SUPREME TRUTH

The word *God* means different things to different people. I wrote this book to explain what God means to me. A lot of people expect that as a Zen Buddhist monk and teacher, I must not believe in God. They've read that Buddhism is a godless religion. And some folks are frightened by this idea. But many, especially the people I meet in my capacity as a Buddhist teacher, are elated by it. They love the idea that they can have a religion without a God.

But in my opinion it's entirely wrong to say that Buddhism is a religion without a God. In fact, it's quite the opposite. To me Buddhism is a way to approach and understand God without dealing with religion.

Right here, at the very beginning of this book, I want to be clear about my position. Alan Watts, author of a number of books about Zen, once said in a lecture,

> I am not a Zen Buddhist; I'm not advocating Zen Buddhism; I'm not trying to convert anyone to it. I have *nothing* to sell: I'm an *entertainer*. That is to say in the same sense that when you go to a concert, and you listen to someone play Mozart, he has nothing to sell except the sound of the music. He doesn't want to convert you to anything, he doesn't want you to join an organization in

favor of Mozart's music as opposed to, say, Beethoven's. And I approach you in the same spirit: as a musician with his piano or violinist with his violin, I just want you to enjoy a point of view which I enjoy.

This is pretty much how I feel. Only I did something that Alan Watts was clever enough not to do. I got ordained a Zen Buddhist monk. What can I say? It seemed like a good idea at the time. And the system needs someone on the inside to irritate it a little bit.

I couldn't care less if you decide to become a Zen Buddhist as a result of reading this book. In fact, I hope you don't. That being said, though, the philosophy and practice associated with Zen Buddhism have been tremendously useful to me; otherwise I'd never have become a monk. I think it might be useful to you too.

But categorizing oneself as a "Zen Buddhist" is absolutely contrary to the spirit of Zen Buddhism. And the organizations claiming to uphold the spirit of Zen Buddhism can be just as silly, hypocritical, and corrupt as any religious institution. Still, unlike Alan, I feel I have little choice but to call myself a Zen Buddhist. I'll address this topic in detail later. But for now I want to concentrate on why I, as a Zen Buddhist, believe in God.

By the way, in this book I will occasionally use the words *Zen* and *Buddhism* somewhat interchangeably. This drives some people bananas. Zen Buddhists often quite arrogantly insist that theirs is the only real kind of Buddhism, while Buddhists of other types just as often insist that it's not. But *Zen* is just the Japanese pronunciation of the Sanskrit word *dhyana*, which means "meditation." So to me Zen Buddhism means Buddhism that involves meditation. Since meditation is the main thing that the historical Buddha taught, I think it's fair to say that anything that calls itself Buddhism and doesn't involve some kind of meditation may not really be Buddhism. So in using the phrase *Zen Buddhism* I'm referring not necessarily to that particular sect and lineage labeled by historians as Zen Buddhism but to all forms of Buddhism that focus on meditation practice, or zazen.

There are many possible answers to the question of whether it's possible to be a Buddhist — Zen or otherwise — and also believe in God. One answer could be that it depends on what you mean by *God*. Another could be that it depends on what you mean by *Buddhist*. A third could be that it depends on what you mean by *believe*. When framing such questions we often take for granted that all parties use the same definitions of the words we choose. But that's not always the case.

I was not raised in a religious family. Oh, I suppose we were nominally Protestant. My dad has a photo that shows me with a group of kids at a local Sunday school. But I couldn't have attended very often since I have no memory of ever having gone at all. I first started getting interested in God when I was about ten years old and the movie *Jesus Christ Superstar* was all the rage.

We were living in Nairobi, Kenya, where my dad worked for the local branch of the Firestone Tire and Rubber Company. He'd been sent there from the home office in Akron, Ohio. I grew up in an Akron suburb until I was about eight and then spent almost four years in Africa. In Africa I made friends with Tommy Kashangaki, whose mother was an American Jewish woman and whose father was Tanzanian. The Kashangakis were raised Catholic. They knew about God. So I used to ask Tommy and his older brother, James, a lot of questions.

What I couldn't get from Tommy, James, or the copy of the *Jesus Christ Superstar* sound track I got for Christmas one year, I learned by reading the children's Bible my mom got us. The whole idea of God was just so weird and fascinating. Some people were sure he* existed. Others were certain he did not. Many, like my parents, didn't know either way.

---

* Of course, God is neither male nor female. But the English language requires us to use a gendered pronoun, and *he* is the common pronoun used when speaking of God. I'm not happy with that. But it's the way things are.

When I thought about God back then I used to imagine him not as a giant white man on a throne in the clouds. I knew even at that age that this was just a metaphorical representation, although I'm sure I couldn't have explained it in those words. Instead I envisioned God as sort of a big, round, shiny entity of some sort. Sort of like the sun but with a personality.

As I grew older, my fascination with God continued. But I became increasingly disgusted with those who claimed to speak for him. We moved back to Ohio when I was eleven, and I soon discovered the amazing world of television evangelism. The idea that there were TV stations entirely devoted to God was pretty intriguing. But it didn't take long for me to figure out that the people who ran these TV stations were as clueless about the real nature of God as anyone else. They were just clever at manipulating people's fears and desires and using God as a way of getting scared and greedy people to send them money.

In high school I discovered books published by the International Society for Krishna Consciousness at a used bookstore called the Book Nook in downtown Wadsworth, Ohio, where I lived. Those Hare Krishna guys also said they knew what God was like. But their version of God was different, at least superficially. God, they said, had a name, which was Krishna, and he had a specific form. He was a handsome purple-skinned Indian youth who could have sex with a thousand girls at a time. The God they talked about at the local Baptist church couldn't do that!

But it soon became apparent that the differences between their God and the one the televangelists spoke about were mostly cosmetic. The God of the Hare Krishnas was just as narrow-minded and vengeful as the one the televangelists believed in. He had a slightly different idea about who to send to hell and why, that's all. Sure, the notion of reincarnation put a different spin on things. But when it came to God, I couldn't find much to like in their version, except that their stories about him were more entertaining.

In college I came across a teacher of Zen Buddhism who had ideas about God that actually made some sense. He showed me a way to see God for myself. But even though I've met God, I still search for him.

My favorite answer to the question of whether it's possible to be a Buddhist and believe in God is "There is no God but he is always with you." I heard this quotation from my first Zen teacher, Tim McCarthy, who learned it from one of his teachers, Sasaki Roshi, a Japanese Zen monk who lives in California. Apparently he was addressing a student of his who believed deeply in God. He wanted her to start seeing God in a different way. So he said this very shocking thing to her, and it worked. I think it expresses the Zen Buddhist approach to the matter of God very succinctly. And not just because it sounds like nonsense.

What you think of as God does not exist. It couldn't possibly exist. No matter what you think of as God, it's an image you've created in your mind. In his book *Buddha Is the Center of Gravity*, Sasaki said, "The God who is standing in front of you as an object says, 'I am your God.' But he is not. Even if that God has great power he is not the real God." And yet there is something powerful and ineffable that is the ultimate ground of all being and nonbeing, and it created you. And some people use the word *God* to talk about that ineffable something. Sometimes I do too.

I've traveled around the world twice in the past two years, and as I write this I'm on my third tour of Europe. I've been speaking to a lot of people about Zen practice while simultaneously deepening my own quest for the true nature of God.

These are some of the questions I've been asking. Can the Zen approach provide an answer to this seemingly irresolvable debate? Can one be an atheist and still believe in God? Is there a way to be a true believer and still doubt? And why frame things in terms of God, anyway? Isn't it just an outmoded concept that only fanatics still talk about?

As a Zen monk* who was born and raised in the United States but who has spent a considerable portion of his life in Japan, I have an unusual take on the matter. Not being raised in any religion, I had no notions about God apart from those I absorbed from the society around me. I was never indoctrinated into any belief system regarding God. So I could look at the various ideas of God that people presented me objectively. But none of them made a lot of sense.

According to D. T. Suzuki, one of the earliest and most influential authors to write about Zen Buddhism in English, "Zen has no God to worship, no ceremonial rites to observe, no future abode to which the dead are destined."† So is Zen some form of spiritual atheism? Writers like Sam Harris and Richard Dawkins have made a compelling case for the new atheist movement. And Karen Armstrong produced a well-reasoned comeback with her book *The Case for God*.

But most of the current debate concerns a very specific definition of God: the Judeo-Christian-Islamic God as framed by contemporary fundamentalists, particularly those in the United States. I'm not sure this debate even makes sense to a lot of people outside North America. Many of the folks I've talked to about it in Europe find the whole argument a little weird.

Yet the cornerstone of the debate is at the core of Western philosophy, which holds sway throughout much of the world, even outside

---

* I'm using the word *monk* as a convenient shorthand to describe myself. But it's a lousy word. It derives from the Catholic tradition and tends to make people assume that Zen monks are like Catholic monks, except that they believe in Buddha instead of Jesus. That's entirely incorrect. As a Zen monk in the Soto tradition I have not taken a vow of celibacy, nor have I committed myself to life in a monastery, just to name two very important differences. Furthermore, Zen is not a religion. So I cannot be considered a member of the clergy. Yet I have taken vows and I have committed myself publicly to uphold the tradition. So in that sense I am a monk. If there were a better single word than *monk* to describe my role in the Zen tradition, I'd use it. Unfortunately, *monk* is the word I'm stuck with.

† He said this in a book called *An Introduction to Zen Buddhism*.

Europe and America. Western philosophy is divided into two compet-
ing ideologies. We are told that we must side either with the materialists, who insist that we are just this body, or with spiritual people, whom
some would file under the category of idealists, who say that we are
just a mind, or a soul, that resides within the body. Even most Eastern
religions insist on this division. The current debate about atheism is
based on this age-old insistence that we must have it either one way or
the other.

This is a big problem with real consequences. In some American
schools arguments rage about whether or not children should study
evolution, while in other parts of the world all forms of scientific in-
quiry are shunned because of the perceived threat they pose to faith in
God. And yet the same people who fear science spread their message
through the sophisticated communication tools that scientific research
has given them. It must be a cause of a great deal of subconscious cognitive dissonance to denounce science on the Internet.

I believe this dissonance lies at the heart of much of the conflict
around us. There is no going back at this point. The genie is out of the
bottle and cannot be returned. Science obviously works. This means that
the materialistic view of the world is, at least in some sense, correct. It
can't be totally wrong or you wouldn't be able to log on to your Face-
book page to say that it's wrong. Does this mean that there is no God?
Does science tell us that all spirituality is just unrealistic wishful thinking?
What about the deep longing in the human heart for something spiritual
in our lives? Must we deny this in order to be rational people?

This was a profound and serious question to me all my life. I knew
science was true, and like many I feared this meant there could be no
God. And yet I felt there was a spiritual dimension to my life that I
could no more deny than I could deny the obvious truth of the scientific
method.

I was deeply involved in the punk scene in my teens and twenties.
So I was already questioning society's basic values, especially those

espoused by religious hypocrites. And as the son of a mother who was dying of a disease I knew I could inherit, from an early age I felt a sense of desperation in my search for a meaning to life. Zen Buddhism has provided me with a way to come to terms with God and to finally settle for myself the question of whether or not God exists.

"There is no God and he is always with you" may sound like a simple non sequitur or a typical pointless Zen riddle. But it expresses the Zen point of view about God very succinctly. Even though what you think of as God can't possibly exist, there is a real spiritual dimension to this world. There is something that can be called God.

The thirteenth-century Zen master Dogen Zenji said, "We know that we ourselves are tools that it possesses within this universe in ten directions because the body and the mind both appear in the universe, yet neither is our self." The word translated here as *it* is the Chinese word *inmo*, which refers to the ineffable substratum of reality, the ground of all being and nonbeing. To me, this is just another way of saying *God*.

I feel it's useful to speak in terms of God because we need to draw attention to the fact that Zen concerns something that is at once very ordinary and very personal and yet very big and very important.

Zen says that both the materialistic and the spiritual view are incomplete and mistaken, that we are neither body nor mind, that our actual reality cannot be defined in such narrow terms. Even the word God is too limiting. Or as Dogen says, "Even the whole universe in ten directions is just a small part of the supreme truth." The supreme truth is, to me, another name for God.

In my early search, the various spiritual ideas I examined about God made no sense. But the idea that human beings were simply walking clumps of dead matter didn't fit my real experience any better. It was my experiences in Zen meditation that made God clear to me in ways that no intellectual expression of God's existence or nonexistence ever could.

In this book I will attempt to make the Zen approach to the question of God comprehensible to a contemporary Western audience steeped in the Judeo-Christian-Islamic traditions. This book is not a religious tract by a true believer trying to convert others to his way of thinking. And it is not meant to quell the fears of those already converted to my religion to assure them they're correct. Rather, it is a straight talk about why this "godless religion" has a lot to say about God.

CHAPTER 1

DEATH IN THE HOLY CITY

Lance Wolf died on the streets of Jerusalem, beaten to death under the very eyes, some would say, of God himself in God's Holy City. Although he was not killed for explicitly religious reasons, Lance was murdered by people who probably thought their version of God was better than his.

I didn't know Lance well. He was a strange guy. I first met him on the third floor of Ibrahim's House of Peace on the Mount of Olives in one of the Palestinian neighborhoods of Jerusalem. He was smoking a cigarette while lying on a pile of blankets on the tiled floor of a bare, dark concrete room.

Ibrahim had taken me upstairs to introduce me and another new lodger at his house to Lance, probably in the hopes that as fellow Americans we could draw Lance out of his shell and maybe get him to come downstairs and eat. Lance was not unfriendly. He sat up on his bedding and chatted enthusiastically. But he wasn't interested in coming downstairs or eating. I couldn't really see his face except when he puffed on his cigarette and the red glow illuminated his gaunt features.

Lance came out of his room a few times later that week, always talking about politics or religion. Nobody I spoke with knew when he'd arrived in Israel or why. A Jew, maybe he was one of those guys who come to Israel hoping for an audience with God. Maybe he was running away from something back home.

Ibrahim's House of Peace is a hostel in a Palestinian village called At-Tur. At-Tur is the kind of place tourists don't usually visit unless they end up there by accident while visiting the nearby scenic overlook from which you can see all of Jerusalem. Or else they wind up there while stopping by the world's oldest Jewish cemetery, where pious folks get buried in the hopes that when the Messiah descends on the Mount of Olives they'll be the first to greet him. You can see the Garden of Gethsemane from there. Some of the olive trees in the garden are more than two thousand years old and were there when the Romans took Jesus away to be crucified. But if they saw what really happened that night they're not telling.

Ibrahim is a short Palestinian man, around seventy years old, with close-cropped white hair and a stubbly white beard. He's a friendly, generous character who for the past thirty years has opened up his home to travelers from all over the world. Anyone can stay at his house for however long she likes — no questions asked. Payment is however much you can afford. There's a collection box next to the kitchen. Nobody asks you to pay, and nobody checks how much you've put in, or even if you've contributed at all.

Ibrahim carries no passport and claims no allegiance to any nation. Yet he travels around the world promoting peace. He has a few favorite travel stories that he repeats over and over to whoever comes around. I think he said he was a Sufi, though someone else at the house told me he wasn't. In any case, he is Muslim, but he believes that all religions are equally valid.

"People who have never been here think there is a wall between the Arabs and the Jews and that we are both dangerous people," Ibrahim says. "We are both really good people." He doesn't see the situation in his homeland as hopeless. "We have a lot of love, which we have learned from our religion, love and peace. A lot of goodness has happened in the land between Jewish and Palestinian brothers, the seeds of Abraham."

His house is like something out of an M. C. Escher painting. Stairways appear out of nowhere and lead to odd places. One led to a window, which you could walk through if you ducked down. A fire escape outside the window got you to the flat roof. In the house, and all over Jerusalem, people have drilled into walls built long before the advent of electricity and modern plumbing to insert plastic ducts through which electrical wiring or water pipes can pass. They look like tentacled alien robots that got frozen while trying to break through the buildings.

The heat was the first thing I noticed about Israel. It slams you hard as soon as you step out of the air-conditioned confines of Ben Gurion Airport. I took a tiny cramped shuttle bus from the airport in Tel Aviv to meet a friend who had the necessary connections to get me into Ibrahim's House of Peace, about which the only thing I knew was that it was cheap. The radio on the bus played Israeli pop songs.

You can walk to the Old City of Jerusalem from Ibrahim's place via a steep, narrow road that winds its way down the Mount of Olives past the Garden of Gethsemane. Lance Wolf probably walked to the Old City the evening he was killed there. Very late that night he was beaten bloody and senseless by a couple of young men when he refused to give them cigarettes. Lance was not the most prudent person. He liked arguing with people. Chances are he was confrontational with those kids and they didn't like it very much. Chances are they were drunk, though the God they most likely believed in forbids drinking.

The streets of the Old City are mostly too narrow for vehicles, and a lot of them are roofed over, so it feels like you're not so much walking through a city as walking through a kind of ancient shopping mall. In fact, I didn't even realize I was walking around the stations of the cross until the second time I went inside the Old City. I'd wanted to see the locations where the key events of Christ's life took place. But you can easily walk by the trinket shops without even knowing that some of the most important places in Western history are right behind them.

I visited the Tomb of the Holy Sepulchre, where they say Jesus was crucified and buried. And I visited the Garden Tomb, where they *also* say Jesus was crucified and buried. The Garden Tomb is an altogether more pleasant place. That's probably because its claim to being the holy site is far more dubious, so fewer people go there. The Church of the Holy Sepulchre is dark and depressing, while the Garden Tomb is located in a cool green park. I like my crucifixion sites pleasant, so I vote for the Garden Tomb as the authentic one.

During my visit to the Garden Tomb I met a couple of Filipino guys who were attempting to make a documentary video that I'm sure was about God. One guy had a little digital camera, and he was using it to film another guy, who would stand in front of the cave in which Jesus was allegedly buried, hold up a red velvet cloth with a cross on it, and get very emotional about it. As I stood and watched, one of the little matronly English ladies who run the place stomped up to him and shouted, "I told you to stop!" He promised her he would. Then as soon as she was out of sight they started filming again. Everyone is crazy for God in Jerusalem. That's what the guy I sat next to on the plane told me. He was an Israeli musician who lived in Tel Aviv. He never went to Jerusalem. The place was too much, he said.

At four each morning I was awoken by prayer calls emanating from the speakers on top of a nearby mosque. "*Allah akbar*," the call begins, "God is great." The voice was tinny and hoarse and very, very loud. The prayer call comes five times every day. The one in the morning includes the line "It's better to pray than to sleep." Is it? I sure didn't think so. The wheezy old voice reminded me of the recordings I used to hear on autumn nights when I lived in Japan, blaring from pushcarts selling roasted sweet potatoes. Except the sweet potato guys have the decency not to wake you up at four in the morning.*

---

* In the Zen tradition we often sit sesshins, intensive periods of concentrated zazen meditation, for three or seven or nine days. When you're at one of those they wake you up with an annoying bell at 4:30 in the morning, or 3:30 at some places. But those you sign up for. I hadn't signed up for this!

For all the prayer calls I heard when I was in Jerusalem, I never saw anyone actually praying. Sometimes you'd see Orthodox Jews walking around with their noses buried in books of scripture, reciting things and paying no attention to the world that God created. I wondered how many of these guys got picked off by cabs every year while walking across the streets peering into their holy books.

The Palestinians I saw in Israel didn't appear to be particularly religious. The conflict between Israelis and Palestinians doesn't seem to be religiously motivated except in a very superficial way. I can't say I'm any kind of an expert. But even just a week in Jerusalem will make at least that much clear.

Many Palestinians who live in Israel, like Ibrahim, are stateless. This is why Ibrahim carries no passport. Yet somehow he manages to travel around the world. It's a big hassle for him to cross borders as an Arab without the proper documents. But he is dedicated to the cause of peace, and he is willing to put up with the hassle.

He says, "As a Palestinian living in Israel I cannot have Israeli citizenship, and as I live in East Jerusalem in Israel I am not legally a Palestinian. I need a visa if I want to make the hajj to Mecca, and it is forbidden for me to go, for example, to Syria or Iraq, because I live in Israel. It is easier for me to travel to Europe or the US than to most Arab countries." If Ibrahim, or any other Palestinian living in Israel, were to leave Israel for more than one year, he would not be allowed to return home. "We don't want the Israeli government to feed us honey and cake," he says. "But we need the freedom and right to live on our land. We ask the government to treat us as people who want to live here and give us rights, for example, for our children to go out to study and come back when they want."*

After Lance was beaten up, Ibrahim stayed by his side in the hospital until he died from his injuries. Lance wasn't a big guy, and he wasn't

---

* All quotations from Ibrahim, other than the things he told me himself, are from his website, http://jerusalempeacehouse.com.

very healthy to begin with. Ibrahim had long been worried that Lance would die in his house.

The British paper *The Daily Mail* described Lance's attackers as "Arab boys between 13 and 15." The boys were later caught and charged with manslaughter. It's safe to assume they were Muslim, at least nominally. But what happened had very little to do with religion in terms of the way most people conceive of it, except in the way that all religions divide humanity and equip individuals to view others as enemies. So, to my way of thinking, this means the attack had everything to do with religion.

Lots of people go to Jerusalem to find God. It's a weird idea that the Creator and Master of the Whole Universe could be found more in one city than another, let alone on planet Earth rather than, say, on Ceti Alpha VI or Tatooine. But, then again, if you believe certain ancient books, God did seem to have a preference for sending his messengers to the area. In my lifelong quest for God, it was only natural that I'd come to Jerusalem.

There is nothing supernatural about the city. But when so many people have, for so many centuries, viewed a certain place as significant, the place itself seems to somehow absorb all that. It's hard not to feel some kind of specialness about Jerusalem. Certainly significant events in human history have occurred there. Whether or not you agree, for example, that the death of Jesus was meaningful in any metaphysical way, you have to admit that it has been given meaning by millions of people. And that's certainly something.

I find the behavior of religious believers to be a special kind of geekiness that leads people to go way overboard, often with tragic consequences. I used to work for a company that made bad Japanese monster movies. Part of my job was to act as a sort of liaison between the company and American and European fans of our films. One thing that always surprised me was that people who are fans of cheap Japanese monster movies will go to monster conventions, and instead of being overjoyed at meeting fellow geeks with whom they have so much in common, they often end up fighting each other over the minutest trivial shit. Godzilla geeks pretty much all hate each other.

Religions work the same way. Christians, Jews, and Muslims — the people who hate one another the most — seem to me like a bunch of geeks who are involved in the same fantasy with only the most negligible of differences, as measured by anyone who doesn't buy into that fantasy. Yet they'll kill each other over these differences. In Jerusalem I had trouble telling Orthodox Jews from Orthodox Muslims from Orthodox Christians. They all cover their bodies in absurd clothing (considering the incredible heat of the place), they all restrict their diets in weird ways, they all obsess over pretty much the same book, they all even say they believe in the same God. And yet they'll turn what look to an outsider such as me like arguments about whether Godzilla has four toes or three* into the kinds of things worth killing for.

Although I believe in God, I can't believe in a God who makes certain cities more sacred than others. Only human beings do such stupid things. God is no more present in the Holy Land of Jerusalem than he is in Bodhgaya, where Buddha was enlightened, or in Mecca, where Muhammad (peace be upon him) first received Allah's prophecies, or in Vrindaban, where Krishna played. He's just as present in Brooklyn and Poughkeepsie and Akron, Ohio.

Or does God even exist at all? Does the concept of existence have any relevance when speaking about God? And is this kind of talk just a lot of hot air for philosophers and guys stoned on too much weed to blow around without any real meaning for the rest of us? Let's take a look at that next.

---

* I swear to God(zilla) I've seen monster movie geeks get into huge rows over this point.

CHAPTER 2

THERE IS NO GOD

While people in Jerusalem, and indeed all over the world, fight and die over which version of God is real, others are just as adamant that there is no God at all. But what does it really mean to say that God exists or does not exist?

"We do not know what God is. God himself doesn't know what he is because he is not anything. Literally God is not, because he transcends being." This very Zennish statement was made in 840 CE by Irish theologian John Scotus Eriugena at the court of the Frankish king Charles the Bald. I came across the quotation in a book called *Dangerous Visions*, a collection of science fiction stories that was put together by Harlan Ellison in 1967. These were, at the time, shocking science fiction tales. Philip K. Dick references Eriugena in the afterword to his story "Faith of Our Fathers," itself a striking science fiction look at religion and God influenced by its author's experiences while he was using LSD.

Eriugena was a fan of the works of a fifth-century CE writer we've come to know as Pseudo Dionysus. He's "pseudo" because, although his works are often attributed to Dionysus, we know that he was not, in fact, the historical Dionysus. Pseudo Dionysus said that "the being of all things is the over-being of God." He viewed God not as a gargantuan granddaddy who lives outside the universe and views it from on high but as the very ground of the reality we live in. This view of God is not unprecedented in the Christian Bible. In Acts 17:27–28 Saint Paul says, "[People] should seek the Lord, if haply they might feel after him, and find him, though he be not far from every one of us: For in him we live, and move, and have our being."*

God does not exist, says Eriugena, because he is beyond existence. To say that he exists is to place him in contradistinction with that which does not exist. But if God is really God, then he cannot be bound by such categories as existence and nonexistence.

This is a nice piece of logic, and I happen to like it quite a bit. But in the end that's all it is. Because in order to agree with the logic, you have to first accept that there is something called God who is infinite and omniscient and transcendent and so on. But what if you don't believe in that in the first place? What if you're coming to this discussion from the standpoint that all matter is essentially dead and that consciousness is just an accident arising from the movement of electricity in the cerebral cells of animals who think far too highly of their own random brain farts?

Pseudo Dionysus has an answer: "Find out for yourself." You cannot answer the question of God's existence or lack thereof through reasoned analysis. So rather than just stopping at a logical explanation of God he goes further. He says, "In the diligent exercise of mystical contemplation, leave behind the senses and the operations of the intellect, and all things sensible and intellectual, and all things in the world of being and nonbeing, that you may arise by unknowing towards the union, as far as is attainable, with it that transcends all being and all knowledge." These instructions sound very much like the ones the Japanese monk Dogen gave seven hundred years later and five thousand

---

* Pretty much all the Bible quotes I'm using in this book come from the King James Version (KJV). I know the KJV translation is now considered by some to be antiquated and often incorrect, but the translation is so much prettier. Whenever I've used quotes from the KJV I've also consulted newer, more reliable translations to be sure the KJV quotations I've used say pretty much the same thing as the more reliable translations.

miles away for sitting zazen meditation. Dogen said, "Do not think of good and bad. Do not care about right and wrong. Stop the driving movement of mind, will, and consciousness. Cease intellectual consideration through images, thoughts, and reflections."

It was these instructions from Dogen and from Pseudo Dionysus (via cheap science fiction paperbacks) that formed the basis for my own quest to understand God. It was clear to me from even the cursory reading I did of the Bible and the Bhagavad Gita, which the Hare Krishnas believed in, that God was not to be found inside books. Books could only explain what other people supposed God might be. Even if they purported to be firsthand accounts from people who had experienced God, they were still the memories of someone else's experience set down in writing. They were not the experience itself. To experience God, if indeed there was a God to be experienced, was up to me.

I felt the effort was worthwhile. This was an important question, and important questions are hard to answer. If God was everywhere, as all the believers said he was, then he was right here. So it made perfect sense to me that one way to meet him was to sit very still and be very quiet — to meditate. Maybe if I stopped paying attention to my own brain farts, I might be able to see God, who, they said, was sitting right in front of me. "If you don't want to be grabbed by God," Zen teacher Jiyu Kennet said, "don't stare at a wall. Definitely don't sit still." I took her nonadvice and sat and stared.

But not everyone is ready to make that terrible leap into the unknown and unknowable. About them Pseudo Dionysus says, "These things are not to be disclosed to the uninitiated, by whom I mean those attached to the objects of human thought." I tend to agree. But let's talk about intellectual justifications for and denials of God for a bit.

In the realm of logic and reason both the proposition that God is real and the proposition that God is unreal can be made to sound convincing. Any freshman philosophy student is familiar with a whole list of pro and con God arguments: the cosmological argument, the ontological argument, the anthropic argument, and so on for God, as well as the argument of inconsistent revelations, the omnipotent paradox, the historical induction argument, and so on against God. You can look all these up on Google if you're really interested. I did and found them mostly beside the point. But if you ask me, the notion that God does not exist seems more compelling in terms of these kinds of logic-based arguments. The pro-God arguments are generally even more flimsy than the ones against God.

Speaking for the logic of science, Stephen Hawking was quoted in the *Huffington Post*[*] as saying that the human brain was like a computer and that "there is no heaven or afterlife for broken-down computers; that is a fairy story for people afraid of the dark." He also stated in the *Telegraph* that God was not necessary to create the universe. "Because there is a law such as gravity, the Universe can and will create itself from nothing. Spontaneous creation is the reason there is something rather than nothing, why the Universe exists, why we exist," he said. "It is not necessary to invoke God to light the blue touch paper and set the Universe going."[†]

Maybe I'm weird. But my own belief in God would not be shaken in the slightest even if it were to be proven beyond any possibility of doubt that the universe did arise from nothing. Because God, to me, is also nothing at all. Which is why I believe in God.

It's possible that Hawking's personal views are not as mechanistic as these sound bites make them seem. After all, in his 1988 book, *A Brief History of Time*, he wrote, "If we discover a complete theory, it would be the ultimate triumph of human reason — for then we should know the mind of God." But I think it's fair to say that his comments above represent the highly materialistic — some might say "physicalist" — standpoint that a lot of people do take on the subject of God. There is a widespread view that our nonphysical experience of the universe is simply the accidental by-product of the way our entirely mechanical brains process information.

---

[*] September 4, 2011, issue.
[†] September 2, 2010, issue.

But believers in God can use logic to push for their views as well. If, for example, examination of the physical world provides no evidence of God, a believer can just say that God is entirely nonphysical and therefore leaves no evidence of his existence in the physical realm apart from the fact that he created it in the first place.

This is why logical arguments for or against the existence of God are largely irrelevant, as far as I'm concerned. In *Star Trek V: The Final Frontier*, Captain Kirk goes rocketing off to the center of the galaxy to find a being that calls itself God. But even when he gets there and meets the guy, it ends up proving nothing at all. That movie was a piece of schlock. But it had a point. Science and logic are never going to prove or disprove the existence of God, at least not to anyone who isn't already inclined to believe or to disbelieve.

Early Buddhist cosmology has some interesting ideas when it comes to the existence of God, as well as of various demons, angels, and other such spiritual beings. The early Buddhists generally accepted much of the cosmology that was current in India at the time Buddhism first came into being.

Many Indians then — and now — accepted the existence of a great number of spiritual beings and realms in which these beings lived. The Buddhists developed a cosmology based on these ideas. There are said to be six realms of existence, which are, from lowest to highest, hell; the realm of hungry ghosts; the realm of asuras (angry demons); the realm of animals; the realm of human beings; and the realm of devas (spirits or gods).

Most of what I know about these realms comes not from my Zen training but from books I've read for personal interest. In fact, neither of my Zen teachers ever required me to read any books at all. In particular my knowledge comes from one very good book called *Buddhist Religions* by Richard H. Robinson, Willard L. Johnson, and Thanissaro Bhikku. As a Zen monk I was never required to believe in or even to know very much about early Buddhist cosmology. It sometimes comes up in the chants we do, such as in the verse chanted before meals during Zen retreats, in which the food is dedicated to the "beings in the six realms." But my two Zen teachers never elaborated very much on these ideas. Neither of them seemed to really believe in these realms, nor have I ever heard any other Zen teachers talk much about such matters. This is a very important manifestation of how Zen Buddhism deals with the matter of cosmology — which is to say that it doesn't deal with it because it doesn't consider cosmology very important.

This is because Zen came rather late in the history of Buddhism. In its march across Asia, Buddhism first picked up a very elaborate cosmology and then mostly discarded it. The Zen teachers I studied with viewed the gods, demons, and their respective realms spoken of in Buddhist texts as primitive descriptions of what we'd now call psychological states.

But for what it's worth, the early Buddhists saw these realms very differently from how the analogous realms that exist within Judeo-Christian-Islamic cosmology are viewed. For example, there isn't just one hell but lots of them. Which one a person ends up in depends on what sort of behavior got him or her there in the first place. There are cold hells like the Blister Hell, where it's so cold you get blisters. And there are hot hells like Crushing Hell, where big boulders smash everybody to jelly over and over. But my favorite Buddhist hell realm is the Hell of Dark Metal, which would be an excellent name for a band. Unlike the Christian hell, these hell realms are not permanent. They're more like purgatory as envisioned by the Catholic Church. You may end up in some kind of hell for a while, maybe even for a very long while, but once the karma that got you there is used up, you get to move on.

The realm of devas is the closest thing the early Buddhists had to an idea of heaven. They accepted the existence of the top tier of gods worshipped by their fellow country people, gods such as Indra and Brahma. Indra functions in many ways very much like Jehovah, in that he rules all the heavens and is chief of all celestial deities. But in the Buddhist version, even Indra is subject to death. He'll be the chief god until he burns out all his godly karma, and then he'll die and someone else will take over the job.

Brahma, another of the earlier Indian gods, is said to be the creator of the universe. But even he, according to the Buddhists, is subject to the law of karma. Like Indra, Brahma will eventually pass away and somebody else will take over his job. To make things even more confusing to those of us who grew up with monotheism, there isn't just one Brahma but several, who each live in their own Brahma realms. Don't ask me to explain because I don't understand it myself.

Indra appears in Buddhist scriptures in a couple of key places. For example, just after Buddha gets enlightened he thinks he ought to keep his discoveries to himself since nobody will understand them. However, Indra comes along and pleads for Buddha to teach the people of the world what he has learned, and Buddha acquiesces.

The authors of the book *Buddhist Religions* bring up a very interesting Buddhist take on the matter of God as creator of the universe and of those of us who inhabit it. At the end of each eon, the entire universe is destroyed. The first being to be reborn is the Great Brahma for the upcoming age. At about the same time that he starts feeling lonesome, other beings that had been destroyed at the end of the previous eon start being reborn. The Great Brahma assumes himself to be their creator, and these newly reborn beings accept him as such.

In his book *Early Buddhism and the Bhagavad Gita*, Kashi Nath Upadhyaya refers to this episode from the early Buddhist sutras. Buddha says there that the Great Brahma looks upon these newly incarnated creatures and thinks, "I am Brahma, the great Brahma, the supreme One, the mighty, the all-seeing the ruler, the lord, the maker, the creator, the chief of all assigning each his place as controller, the father of all that are and are to be."

Yet this is just a delusion. The Great Brahma and his creations are all subject to the law of cause and effect. According to one sutra referenced in the book *Buddhist Religions*, the Great Brahma is depicted by the Buddha as "a pompous hypocrite hiding his ignorance from his adoring retinue."

You can see from these examples that when Buddhism addresses the topic of God, it's not addressing quite the same concept as the all-powerful monotheistic God posited by Jews, Christians, and Muslims, whom they might view as another name for the delusional Great Brahma. Much of the Indian thought about God appears in a series of scriptures called the Upanishads, as well as in the Bhagavad Gita (Song of God). Some of the Upanishads were composed before Buddha's time, while several others were composed later. The dates for the Bhagavad Gita are disputed. Some claim that it predates Buddha by thousands of years. Others believe that while the original version of the Gita may predate Buddha, the version we now possess has been revised and shows the influence of Buddhism.

Both the Upanishads and the Bhagavad Gita speak of two aspects of God. Confusingly, these aspects go by very nearly the same name. Brahma is the personal aspect of God, while Brahman — with an *n* at the end — is the impersonal. Brahman is absolute reality beyond all contradictions. You can't say what it is, only what it is not. Indian religious people often use the phrase *neti-neti*, or "not this, not this" to refer to the string of negative statements one must make when talking about Brahman.

In *Early Buddhism and the Bhagavad Gita*, Upadhyaya pulls several adjectives from the Bhagavad Gita that are used to describe Brahman. It is "existent as well as non-existent," it is, "incomprehensible, unthinkable, indefinable and unknowable." It is "the knower as well as that which is known." It is "knowledge, the object of knowledge and the goal of knowledge." The Gita says that "though it appears to have the qualities of all senses, it is devoid of all senses." Additionally, it is "inside as well as outside of all beings, it is moving as well as unmoving . . . it is far away and yet quite near."

The Bhagavad Gita attempts to resolve the contradictions between the impersonal and the personal aspects of God by merging them within the person of Krishna, the central character in its narrative. Krishna is the personal manifestation of the impersonal Brahman. This is the same Krishna whose name is chanted by guys with funny haircuts dressed in orange robes you can see at airports and bus stations all over the world, the ones whose books I read when I was in high school. In a way this idea of Krishna is much like the later Christian idea of Christ, God in human form.

It's all extremely confusing, if you ask me. But I bring it up because it's important for Western readers to understand that Buddhism comes out of a philosophical/religious tradition that is quite different from the one most of us are familiar with.

Similarly, much of the currently in vogue neoatheism attacks a concept of God that not too many believers in God actually accept. Of course, there really are people out there who believe in a very simplistic notion of God as a giant Santa Claus–type figure who sits on a throne way up in heaven somewhere above the clouds. And those guys like to make their voices heard. But I don't think those people really speak for many more others whose idea of God is far subtler, or for those who refuse to even conceive of God not out of laziness but because they believe, like Pseudo Dionysus, that God is beyond any concept they can come up with, anyway.

I've said it before in my other books, and I'll say it again. If God is a big white man with a beard who sits on a throne up in the sky, then there is no God, as far as I'm concerned. The subtler notions of God are more difficult to refute. But if it ends up being just a matter of moving God farther and farther away to prevent us from finding out he doesn't exist, then I still don't believe in God.

And yet something in my real experience leads me to say I believe in God, mostly because of almost three decades of what Pseudo Dionysus called "leaving behind the senses and the operations of the intellect," my daily practice of what is called zazen in Japanese, a type of silent and undirected meditation. Those of you without such a background might be skeptical that anything can be learned through such methods. I understand. But I also know that nothing I can say will convince you if you haven't done this yourself.

But you're still reading. So maybe you want to know what conclusions I've come to and why.

CHAPTER 3

...AND HE IS ALWAYS WITH YOU

For a lot of people the biggest argument for the existence of God is the existence of everything else. All the stuff that surrounds us — the stars, the planets, the galaxies, the idiots who drive gas-guzzling SUVs — all of it must have come from somewhere, right? If everything has a cause, then there must be some ultimate cause that precedes all other causes.

The most popular argument based on this reasoning is called the "watchmaker hypothesis." It goes like this. If you were to come across a watch and you'd never seen one before, you'd know instantly that someone had made it. Nothing as complex as a watch could just pop into being on its own. And the universe is much more complex than a watch. Therefore, God is the great watchmaker in the sky. Or something like that.

There's also an argument making the rounds on the Interwebs about bananas. Bananas, it is said, are proof of God's existence because they fit perfectly inside the hands of monkeys and humans who eat bananas. Therefore God made bananas for us to eat. And, I suppose, anything that doesn't fit in our hands must not be proper food for us.

Yet the watchmaker argument, the banana argument, and the many other arguments like them fall apart when you ask what caused God.

Because the entire premise rests on the notion that everything must have a cause. You can't resolve an argument based on the premise that *everything* has a cause by postulating some being — God — that has no cause.

Still, the universe must have some kind of cause. Right?

This is how I thought of it for most of my young life. I figured there had to be a God simply because everything has *some* kind of a cause. I wasn't convinced by the watchmaker argument except in a very broad sense. I was undecided as to whether or not God sat around and tinkered with things in order to make the universe, like a watchmaker making a watch. Where would he get the stuff he needed to make the universe? I believed, and still believe, in evolution and in the scientific method. And yet it seemed there must be some ultimate cause. Furthermore, it was attractive to think of that ultimate cause as an intelligent being of some sort.

And yet, like everyone else who thinks along these lines, I got stuck. The thinking is similar to what the fictional heavy metal guitarist Nigel Tufnel says in the movie *This Is Spinal Tap*: "If the universe isn't infinite, then what's stopping it? And what's behind what's stopping it?" You're faced with infinite regression. This question seems insurmountable. And most arguments I've heard end right there. It's a big wall that we can't get over, around, under, or through.

The problem is time. We all make some very definite assumptions about time, and we believe in these assumptions absolutely, without ever really examining them. Time flows in one direction and one direction only. We can see that. Our cars get rustier over time. Our laptops fail. We get older, not younger. So the ultimate cause of everything must lie in the very distant past because that's the only place, as far as we can see, that it could possibly be. Science searches for the ultimate cause in the big bang some fourteen billion years or so ago. We've been trying to detect the faint echoes of this enormous explosion by scanning the farthest reaches of outer space.

Yet some contemporary cosmologists think the big bang may not actually be the ultimate cause. Perhaps a universe of some sort existed before the big bang that gave birth to our universe. That previous universe may have contracted to a point and then burst out to become ours. Maybe these oscillations go on infinitely back in time. Although some say time itself has no meaning when applied to events like the big bang and whatever may have come before. And now some are saying that it wasn't a big bang at all, that this universe is what happens when you leave nothing alone for long enough. It has to turn into something. It's all incredibly confusing.

In any case, it looks like most people see the ultimate cause of everything as an event — or perhaps a being who caused that event — a long, long time ago. You could, I suppose, say that there is no ultimate cause. And some people do. But that seems to be one of those arguments that explain nothing.

You could also say that it doesn't matter since very likely there's no way we could ever know anything about the ultimate cause of everything. So we might as well just forget it. Sometimes it seems like this is the Buddhist solution. But that's not really it.

It's not impossible to understand or even experience the very moment of universal creation. You just have to put aside your habitual understanding of time.

Dogen Zenji, that thirteenth-century Japanese Buddhist monk I mentioned earlier, was a brilliant writer who left behind a mountain of philosophical and poetic works about Zen practice and Buddhist thought. His written works form the basis of the style of Zen that I have studied and practiced for nearly thirty years now. His writings are not considered divinely inspired or infallible. But they are damned good. I don't think anyone since him has really written as lucidly on the subjects he addresses. His writings are based both on a thorough knowledge of Buddhist texts and on his personal experience with the practice. They're a mixture of philosophical analysis and his unique understanding gleaned from decades of intense meditation. Warning: I'm going to refer to Dogen and his writings a lot in this book.

Dogen writes about something he calls "being-time." To him, existence and time are one and the same. And that doesn't just mean you exist at this moment and this moment only. In a chapter called "*Uji*," or "Being-Time," in his masterwork *Shobogenzo*, "Treasury of the True Dharma Eye," he says, "Because [real existence] is only this exact moment, all moments of existence-time are the whole of time, and all existent things and all existent phenomena are time." He asks us to "pause to reflect whether or not any of the whole of existence or any of the whole universe has leaked away from the present moment of time."

I've reflected on that a lot. And it seems to me that time can never really "leak away" from this moment. What exists right here and now contains everything that came before it and everything that will come after. There isn't anywhere else for time or matter to go.

The infinite past and the infinite future are contained within this moment right now. In the book *Zen Mind, Beginner's Mind* Shunryu Suzuki quotes Dogen as saying that time flows from present to past. Suzuki might be referring to this statement, also from the same chapter of *Shobogenzo*:

> Existence-time has the virtue of passing in a series of moments. That is to say, from today it passes through a series of moments to tomorrow; from today it passes through a series of moments to yesterday; from yesterday it passes through a series of moments to today; from today it passes through a series of moments to today; and from tomorrow it passes through a series of moments to tomorrow. Because passage through separate moments is a virtue of time, moments of the past and present are neither piled up one on top of another nor lined up in a row.

Dogen further states, "We should learn in practice that without the momentary continuance of our own effort in the present, not a single dharma nor a single thing could ever be realized or could ever continue from one moment to the next." All of existence and all of time is our own creation, even as we are created by all of existence and all of time. The cause of all existence, of everything that ever was, is, or will be, he says, is *us*. The center of the universe, and the center of time, the beginning of creation is *you*. Everything radiates from that center and returns to it.

Dogen was questioning our everyday notions of time and of God. The common understanding of time was pretty much the same in thirteenth-century Japan as it is for us today. Dogen saw things very differently. Or perhaps we should say he "sees things very differently," since whoever or whatever Dogen was is still with us today even though we can't send Dogen an email and ask him to explain himself.

Our experience of real time sometimes stands at odds with what we think we know about how time works. Future events seem to influence the present. We appear to remember things that haven't happened yet. These kinds of occurrences are sometimes classified as paranormal. But ask around, and you'll discover that almost everyone has experienced these things at some point or another.

I don't like to get too deeply into such things. Because whenever you do, people just won't let it go. We're fascinated by the supposed mysticalness or paranormality of such phenomena. Yet all of us experience them. Everyone I've ever talked to about the subject can recall instances when they've known about something before it actually came to pass. I think it's a universal phenomenon.

Science seems to be making inroads into exploring some of this. In the book *God and the New Physics*, Paul Davies says, "Quantum theory requires a sort of reversed-time causality inasmuch as an observation performed today can contribute to the construction of reality in the remote past." It's mind-blowing stuff, to be sure. I don't really get it myself. So I am supremely unqualified to explain it.

If being is time, then our existence here and now is the moment of creation. Not conceptually or metaphorically, but *actually* in practice and experience. The conceptual distance we place between our existence here and now and God's moment of creation all those millennia ago may be just a figment of our imaginations.

Again, there is nowhere for the moment of creation to have leaked away to. The difference between time and things is a useful illusion that helps us organize stuff in our heads, but that's all it is. We are not beings who move through time. We are time itself. And the only real time is this moment. The fact that real existence is only this moment is easy to see. Although we treat the past as if it is a real thing, the past is nowhere to be found. We can only find traces of it in the present moment — photographs, documents, memories, and so on. The future too is contained in the present moment. Nothing can happen in the future that doesn't depend on the conditions that exist right now. You can't fly away under your own power because you were not born as a bird. Nothing can happen except what's possible based on the present state.

We could follow this idea into an argument about whether everything is determined or if free will is possible. The Buddhist answer is that it is both, and therefore neither. Buddhism is full of contradictions like this because Buddhism acknowledges that real life is often contradictory. Our brains are capable of seeing things only one way at a time. But real life has it all ways all the time.

Nishijima Roshi, the Zen teacher who ordained me, had a favorite way of explaining this. He would say that the present moment is like a pearl balanced on the edge of a razor blade. The pearl may fall to the left side or to the right, or it may stay balanced where it is. At the present moment things are only one way. In the future that pearl will be on one side or the other, or it'll stay put. But right now, at the razor's edge of time, it has the potential to go in any of these directions. Once it has made its choice, if pearls can be said to make choices, it will have a different set of potentials. So at this moment we are free to do whatever we choose, given the constraints that our past has placed on us.

So did God create the universe? I think this is an impossible question. Not because it's too big or too far removed or anything like that.

It's an impossible question because it frames the problem in an impossible way. It says you have God, which is one thing, and you have the universe, which is another. You're asking whether one thing created the other thing the way, say, Da Vinci created the *Mona Lisa*.

But Da Vinci didn't really create the Mona Lisa, at least not in the sense that believers in God say God created the universe. Da Vinci didn't conjure up the canvas the *Mona Lisa* is painted on. He didn't snap his fingers and make the paint he used appear out of thin air. He didn't twitch his nose and make the model who sat for the portrait materialize in his studio. Da Vinci put all those things together in a unique way. In terms of how human beings tend to view things, he is the creator, but he is not the ultimate creator of the painting.

To say that God created the universe you would have to say that God is the universe. Otherwise, you have to say that once upon a time God found some stuff and made a universe out of that stuff. If God is everything, then what's the stuff? If God created the stuff, what did he make it out of? I guess you could say he just magically caused it to be there since he can do anything. But that doesn't seem logical, especially if you're trying to trace creation back to its ultimate source. When Nishijima Roshi was questioned about God he always said, "God is the universe, the universe is God."

Some people would say that makes Nishijima a pantheist. A pantheist is someone who believes that God and the universe, or nature, are identical. In his book *The God Delusion* the überatheist Richard Dawkins described pantheism as "sexed-up atheism." But Nishijima is not a pantheist, and neither am I. Buddhism is something a bit different. To sum it up by calling it pantheism is much too simple.

Most people who espouse pantheism appear to think that they know what the universe is or at least that they have a pretty good idea. The universe is this vast place full of stars and galaxies and maybe Mr. Spock and Wookies and all kinds of stuff. The sum total of all that stuff they call "God" because to call it anything less would be to remove its grandeur and wonder.

This is all perfectly fine as far as it goes. But I feel we have to push things even further. Just because we have names for the stuff of the universe and a vague understanding of how gravity works and how atomic forces interact and whatnot doesn't mean we really grasp the totality of what that stuff actually is. Gravity is mystical. Atomic forces are mystical. This place we're living in is as crazily improbable as Oz or Alice's Wonderland. It really, seriously, is.

Furthermore, pantheism is speculative and intellectual. It's based on concepts and ideas about things, whereas Buddhism is based on real experience.

Near the beginning of chapter 2 of *The God Delusion*, Richard Dawkins defines what he calls the "God Hypothesis": "There exists a superhuman, supernatural intelligence who deliberately designed and created the universe and everything in it, including us." Dawkins advocates an alternative view that says, "Any creative intelligence, of sufficient complexity to design anything, comes into existence only as the end product of an extended process of gradual evolution. Creative intelligences, being evolved, necessarily arrive late in the universe and therefore cannot be responsible for designing it." He finishes by saying, "God in the sense defined is a delusion."

I would have to agree with him there. In the sense that Dawkins has defined God, God is definitely a delusion. I do not believe in a superhuman supernatural intelligence who created the universe a long time ago. And yet I do believe in God.

Dawkins's argument against God involves linear time. I'm not going to invoke what appears to be the easiest argument a believer in God could come up with against this. That easy argument would be to say that God created time as well and can therefore do whatever he wants with it, including violate its unalterable forward motion. The British theologian Richard Swinbourne is quoted in Dawkins's book as saying, "God is not limited by the laws of nature; he makes them and he can change or suspend them — if he chooses." In other words, God made the steenking law of time, he don't need to obey it!

I won't invoke that because it's a silly argument. It brings the whole matter back down to a debate about concepts. In that sense, Dawkins's argument wins because his is based on observation of the real world, while invoking a God who can violate the forward motion of time just asks us to speculate about something that really can't be proven or disproven.

I do not think that the quotations I've chosen from Dogen can be viewed as the same kind of speculation. Dogen is writing from experience, not from speculation or consideration. The type of meditation Dogen did is not a practice of sitting quietly and thinking things through; rather, it is a practice of allowing all thought to dissipate. In doing this practice, one can enter a state of pure observation. One begins to see what all our thoughts really are — even the most satisfyingly logical and rational ones. As Led Zeppelin said, "Sometimes all of our thoughts are misgiven." Dogen would agree and add that the word *sometimes* should be removed.

Dawkins's book, like so many others both for and against the idea of God, stays purely in the realm of the intellect. Granted, Dawkins does at least back up his intellectual arguments with scientific observations. But even scientific observations belong to the realm of the intellect. They are the intellect's response to stimulation of the senses.

What we are dealing with in Zen is something entirely different. To a person who has never known anything other than the stimulation of the senses and the intellect's response to them, the very idea that there could be anything beyond that seems absurd. And unjustifiable. Then again, to someone who has never been trained in mathematics, the insights that can be gleaned by skillfully manipulating equations also seem absurd and unjustifiable.

But our real experience includes things that the senses cannot perceive and that the intellect cannot comprehend. Nishijima was once asked if a person can notice her own enlightenment. He said, "No."

This also seems absurd. But Nishijima was speaking not from reasoned analysis but from personal experience. That's a very different basis to speak from. Yet we can say a few things about enlightenment, and I'd like to start by saying something about what enlightenment is not.

CHAPTER 4

SEEING GOD THE QUICK, EASY, AND EFFECTIVE WAY!

Supposedly, 2,500 years ago, a man named Siddhartha or Gautama or Shakyamuni — the guy had a lot of nicknames — sat under a tree for a long time until he experienced something that later writers called enlightenment. In Japan they use the word *satori*, which is derived from the verb *satoru*, meaning "to realize." What precisely was realized by Siddhartha under his tree is usually left unspoken. But after he realized it he was called Buddha, the Awakened One.

Words like *enlightenment* and *satori* are tricky. They're imprecise at best. The word *satori* is foreign to us, so we have no idea what it means until someone comes along and gives us an English equivalent. And the word *enlightenment* conjures up images of the Enlightenment Era of the seventeenth and eighteenth centuries, when European intellectuals discovered rationality. But it has nothing to do with that.

I think it would be better for us as Westerners to start using that dangerous and divisive word *God* when we talk about what happened to Buddha all those centuries ago and what continues to happen to contemporary people who follow his way. Let me try and explain why.

An argument exists that goes something like this: 1) The goal of meditation practice is to reach enlightenment. 2) As with any goal, it is better to reach this goal as quickly and easily as possible. 3) Indians in

Buddha's time couldn't get anywhere as fast as Americans can today, so we ought to be able to get to enlightenment much faster and much more easily than they did. Therefore, 4) try my special new course for a low, low introductory fee, order before midnight tonight! Dozens of these courses are available. Just check the back pages of any new age or Buddhist magazine. One of my favorites advertises itself as an "elegant, easy to use, easy to duplicate and quick way to bring about a very deep powerful transformation." Another pitch says, "You can't afford to miss this opportunity to work closely with [Name Withheld] Roshi, where you will realize a deep experience of True Self, a profound state of samadhi and an unconditional faith in what is." That one costs $5,000.

If you think of what Gautama accomplished and what Buddhists aspire to today in terms of seeing God rather than in terms of getting enlightened, it might be easier to understand why quick, easy, and effective enlightenment is so utterly impossible. When we phrase it in terms of enlightenment, we're dealing with pretty much a blank slate as far as the Western mind-set is concerned. We don't really have any idea what this "enlightenment" thing is except that we think it must be pretty nice. When you use trendy words derived from pop psychology like *transformation*, or Sanskrit words like *samadhi*, things get even murkier.

But if you put it in terms of seeing God face-to-face, that changes everything. Our culture is steeped in traditions that emphasize the difficulty and struggle necessary to attain an audience with God, from St. Augustine's famous breakdown to Mother Teresa's well-documented struggles to see God. We're very much aware that reaching God is never quick and easy.

We know that no method of reaching God could ever be so effective that anyone could do it, regardless of whether the person had any real longing to be in the presence of God or was just somebody who happened to walk in off the street with enough money to pay for some "see-God-right-now" seminar. And yet some of the schemes advertised in the magazines imply that a real enlightenment experience can be had quickly and painlessly, even by someone who has at best a passing interest in it.

It amazes me to watch video clips in which the ballroom of a fancy hotel is filled to capacity with people clapping and cheering for some guy who promises them that they'll experience "nothing short of the essential secret of the universe" — to directly quote one of the videos I have seen — in mere minutes. I'm not sure what kind of "essential secret of the universe" is on offer there, but God is not that cheap.

This is one reason that I'm trying to introduce the word *God* into the Western Buddhist dialogue. The word *enlightenment*, or substitutes such as *transformation*, seems to suggest a psychological state that one might induce with some kind of seminar or fancy technique or drugs. If we start talking in terms of "seeing God," it might become clearer to everyone that we're talking about something much grander and much more difficult.

Zen Buddhists often don't like the word *God*. But they do like the word *satori* (and its cousins, *kensho* and *enlightenment*). But to me, the word *satori* is as problematic as the word *God*. No one knows quite what *satori* is. But those who use the word have a lot of vague ideas about it. For all the imagery they surround the word *satori* with, they might as well be talking about a giant white man on a throne in the sky who rules the universe.

On the other hand, *God* is a loaded word — and that's precisely why it's so useful. I know it's a stretch to think of the Buddhist idea of enlightenment in terms of the Christian concept of seeing God. But we need to get a handle on what we're talking about here before going on.

To get a grip on what Buddhism is actually about we need a word that's bigger than *enlightenment*, that's bigger than *satori*. We need a word that evokes something more than a method for reducing stress, like everybody's new favorite word, *mindfulness*. We need a word that points to something grander than the kind of "essential secret of the universe" that you can get in a few minutes, even if you're only mildly interested.

God demands a lot more of you than that. He hasn't got time to hang out with someone who only wants to see him so that he can tell his friends he met somebody famous. The paparazzi can't get a photo of God going out to buy kitty litter and showing a bit of cellulite on his legs. He's a lot more difficult to reach than that. You've really got to want to see him, and you've got to be willing to put in the effort it's going to take.

In other words, seeing God is anything but quick and easy.

I once read a book called *Zig Zag Zen* in which a number of people talk about their belief that psychedelic drugs will do for you in a few minutes what it takes those poor saps who do meditation practice decades to achieve. Drugs are often touted as one of the best of the various quick, easy, and effective methods for meeting God. In the book Charles Tart, renowned American psychologist and parapsychologist and one of the founders of the field of transpersonal psychology, says, "Meditation was far more difficult than I imagined, and a lot of meditating was spent daydreaming, rebuking myself for daydreaming and getting nowhere. It's clear that many of us Westerners have such complex psychological dynamics that it is very difficult to quiet and discipline our minds enough to make any real progress along the meditative path."

This is racist nonsense. The idea that there is any difference between the "Eastern mind" and the "Western mind" in terms of the difficulty of meditation is a pervasive fantasy that contemporary Westerners use as an excuse to drop their meditation practice and look for something easier. In the Victorian era certain European and American people liked to talk about the "Oriental mind." The Oriental mind was said to lack intellectual ability, to be "low, tame and undecided with few strong lights and shades in it," according to a man named John Davy, who studied Asian cultures in the nineteenth century. This sounds like what Mr. Tart is contrasting his own much more complex Western mind to. It's incredible how supposedly enlightened liberal people continue to spout the same sorts of ideas as an excuse for laziness.

The psychological dynamics of Western people are no more complex than those of anyone else.

People are always complaining that their minds are too busy to do meditation. Your mind is not too busy to do meditation. I don't care who you are or how busy your mind is. Your mind and Buddha's mind are equally busy. Meditation is hard for everyone who does it. Everyone. If it wasn't difficult to sit still and be quiet, they wouldn't build giant statues commemorating people whose main claim to fame is that they could sit still and be quiet. It's hard work. But you can do it.

One of the things that makes a person's mind seem "too busy for meditation" is the way we are constantly agitating our brains with unnecessary information and stimulation. It's like sitting there poking your eye with your finger over and over and then complaining that you can't see clearly.

If you pay the least bit of attention to what those ancient Asian people who did meditation said about their practice, you will see right away that even the sages of old had a very hard time with it. Why do you think we have all those stories about Buddha wandering as a naked acetic, sleeping on piles of bones, and starving himself nearly to death? Why do you think we have stories about Bodhidharma* sitting stock-still and staring at the damp walls of a cold cave in the dark mountains until his arms and legs fell off (they didn't really, but that's the way the story gets told)? Why do you think Dogen risked his life to travel to China on a rickety ship in a stormy sea in order to find the real source of meditative practice, even after he'd spent a decade in a Japanese monastery? Can anyone honestly think that this stuff was easy for them because of their psychologically uncomplicated Eastern minds? Bodhidharma and Dogen did not just assume the lotus posture and float off into the clouds.

If anything, meditation is easier for modern Westerners than it

---

* A sixth-century Indian monk who traveled to China and founded Chan Buddhism, which the Japanese later called Zen Buddhism.

was for those Eastern people of long ago. Sure, they weren't dealing with the annoying noise of traffic in the streets. But they *were* dealing with bands of robbers armed with swords and daggers who frequently looted their temples and slaughtered everyone inside. They were dealing with growing their own food, since there wasn't a Whole Foods supermarket down the street. They were dealing with wars and revolutions. Their lives were way harder than ours.

I've gone through multiday retreats where, after a couple of days, it's all I can do just to stay in the temple. I desperately want out. I have yet to actually run away from a retreat, though I have come very close. This still happens, even now that I am a fancy Zen monk and often the leader of the retreat. When it does happen, I have to just sit there as still as possible and make a show of doing my meditation. That's all part of the practice.

But often it's when things get desperate, after hours and hours, or days and days of sitting, that something will spontaneously start to open up. I'll suddenly be confronted with a new aspect of reality. In the ancient sutras they often compare the world to a kind of multifaceted jewel. And sometimes in the deep, deep depths of a miserably long sitting retreat, you start seeing more of these facets.

I wish I could explain what this is like, but I really can't. Whenever I have tried to set it down on paper it just comes out like bad poetry, or like the things you might find on a spoken-word album by Jim Morrison during his really heavy acid days.

When people hear about this process they sometimes make the mistake of negating the initial difficult part. They want to get the reward of seeing God without putting in the effort of getting to where God is. This is understandable. We live in a society that gives its members lots of rewards that they didn't really have to work too hard for.

You can have the experience of being on top of Mount Hood by paying someone to take you up there in a helicopter. But it would not be the same experience as climbing the mountain yourself. Even the view you got when you landed in your helicopter wouldn't be like the view a tired and ecstatic climber gets.

And consider this. Meditation in its barest form is *already* a technique for making what ought to be very hard a lot easier. We are all dealing with hundreds of thousands of years of built-up conditioning. As soon as we're born we start absorbing the collective conditioning the human species has accreted over its entire history on Earth. The fact that we can get through this stuff in a mere decade or two is pretty incredible.

It's all up to you to put in the work. Nishijima Roshi told me years ago that I could see God if I really wanted to. I didn't believe him. Oh, I *wanted* to believe. But I wasn't even convinced there was a God to see in the first place.

Plus, who sees God? Mystics in caves and crazy televangelists, that's who. I wasn't ready to move to a cave. And I sure as hell did not have any interest in becoming one of those horrible people who run around talking and even writing books about how they've seen God.

And yet here I am, typing one of those awful tomes about how I met the Lord. Ugh. Let me tell you about it anyway. First we have to go to Detroit.

CHAPTER 5

MY MEETING WITH GOD, OR ENLIGHTENMENT PORN

Detroit looks like something out of one of those sci-fi movies set after the collapse of human civilization. Once home to nearly two million people, Detroit now has a population that is less than half that. Whole skyscrapers stand empty, some covered in graffiti up to their highest floors. Multilane roads that used to be full of traffic are now mostly empty. The crime rate is so bad that at a rally on October 17, 2012, the Detroit Police Officer Association passed out flyers warning visitors that they entered Detroit "at their own risk." It's a scary place.

I was invited to Detroit by Vince Anila, whose Buddhist name is Koho. He's the head of a Korean-style Zen temple called Still Point in one of the city's roughest areas. Vince assured me that as long as I was careful I'd be fine walking around the neighborhood. And I was. People do still live in Detroit, and not all of them are thugs and criminals. Vince has made a nice garden of serenity in a tough town. I've visited several times and it's always a lot of fun. A little scary, sure. But so are a lot of cities.

I gave several talks about Zen the week I was in Detroit. I also played a show with the hardcore punk band I play bass in, Zero Defex. We used to play in Detroit back in the 1980s when, unbelievably, it was an even scarier place than it is now. Back then we'd pile four bands, along with our equipment and girlfriends, into a rusted-out Econoline van and drive six hours from Akron, Ohio, to do a show in Detroit. Then we'd load everyone and everything back into the van and drive six hours to arrive back in Akron around dawn.

This time I traveled by train to Detroit from another Zen gig in Montreal. The next day I woke up before dawn and did 108 prostrations to Buddha, which is what the folks in the Korean style of Zen Buddhism do every morning. After that I led a daylong silent Zen retreat. When night fell, I made my way to the Magic Stick nightclub right in front of Tiger Stadium, and Zero Defex rocked out with the Amino Acids, a local surf-punk act. Loud never sounds so loud as when you've spent a whole day being quiet.

The following morning I got to sleep in. But that night I had another lecture to do. After that talk a guy came up to me and told me that he'd been really moved by my first book, *Hardcore Zen*, especially the part about my encountering an apparition near a lake.

The part where I encountered a *who* by a *what*?

I had no idea what he was going on about. There's nothing about encountering apparitions or even about lakes in any of my books. But he was emphatic that it was *Hardcore Zen* he was referring to. Finally, after we had chatted for a while, I figured out what he was talking about.

In the book I mentioned crossing a footbridge over a narrow section of the Sengawa River on my way to work one day and there encountering a glimpse of God — though I described it a bit differently. In my reader's mind the river became a lake, which is one level of misunderstanding. But it was a whole other level of misunderstanding to read what I tried to describe about my experience that day as an "encounter with an apparition."

This was not the first time that particular part of the book had been misinterpreted. Clearly I made a mess of things. I've come to understand that one can only make a mess of such things by attempting to write about them. But since I'm writing here about God and what God means in terms of Zen practice I thought I needed to address that incident again. No doubt I will make a mess of things again.

There is a style of writing in books on spirituality that I like to call "enlightenment porn." My friend Jim Millar, formerly the guitarist of the Zen Luv Assassins, used to talk about what he called "guitar porn."* He was talking about magazines with glossy photos of rare and beautiful guitars whose appeal to guitar players is precisely the same as the appeal of porn to just about everyone else. They incite you to lust after things that are not yours and never will be. The object of guitar porn is to get you to spend money on both the porn itself and other guitars that are like the ones shown in the porn.

Enlightenment porn functions much the same way as guitar porn. Enlightenment porn comes mainly in the form of books whose centerpieces are stories of the authors' enlightenment experiences. In hushed and reverent tones the author tells you about how he was in a hut in the deep canyons of Tibet or perhaps on a mountain peak in the Mojave Desert, when all of a sudden he became one with the universe. The story is intended to make you lust after an experience just like the one you're reading about. The author very often hopes you will pay a handsome sum for this privilege, usually at a seminar advertised in the back pages.

In the Soto tradition it is seen as a mistake to talk about these so-called enlightenment experiences publicly. All Dogen, the founder of our tradition, says about his own enlightenment experience is that while he was at Tendo Nyojo's temple in China he experienced "the dropping off of both body and mind." He gives no further details. But, of course, all of his writing is in some respects the story of what he experienced that day.

I, on the other hand, stupidly decided to write about what had happened to me that day by the Sengawa River. I spoke to my teacher Nishijima Roshi about it and showed him what I had written. He

---

* I guess a lot of people use this phrase to refer to a lot of stuff these days. But I heard it from Jim first.

seemed to think it was okay, so I published it. But probably Nishijima already knew what I needed to find out through experience. In the end, I inadvertently created my own piece of enlightenment porn. This may be why that book still sells pretty well.

I myself had read my share of enlightenment porn just after I started doing Zen practice. In particular, I read a book called *The Three Pillars of Zen* by Philip Kapleau, in which the author reproduces the diary entries made by several Zen students about their enlightenment experiences. Just like what happens when you look at a nice juicy piece of that other sort of porn, I wanted one of those experiences for myself. As a matter of fact, this was one of the things that made Zen appeal to me more than the other approaches to God I had been exposed to. Zen seemed to offer you a chance to actually see God for yourself.

Granted, lots of other religions make this claim too. But in those cases, the evidence seemed weaker. There were evangelical Christians who said you could meet God. But they said it would happen after you died and only if you had followed the vague plan laid out in the Bible. And it was always impossible to know if you were even getting that plan right. In their scheme of things, it seemed very likely that a person could think she was doing the right thing all along, only to be told after she'd died that, no, she'd blown it and was therefore damned to hell for eternity. Sorry. You should have read the fine print!

The Hindus also had their ways of experiencing God for themselves. But their methods always seemed too elaborate and painful. Guys would starve themselves or undergo really severe, intense training. You'd see paintings of yogis who'd sat still so long that vines had grown over their bodies, and their eyes were bugged out, and their bones were showing through their skin because they hadn't eaten anything but raisins for twelve years or something. It was pretty insane. Then you had the Hare Krishnas, who preached exactly the same thing as the Christians — that if you did everything right, maybe you'd get to see God after you were dead. But again, you could never be certain you were doing everything right by God until such time as you got to meet him. Or not. And some of their guys seemed to get in even more trouble in terms of sex and money scandals than the Christians.

None of that appealed to me. I am not a gambler. Nor do I want to run off to the secluded mountains and drive myself so crazy with isolation, lack of food, and bizarre mental and physical gymnastics that I start believing my own hallucinations.

Zen seemed to offer a middle way. It required me to put in a certain degree of hard effort. Yet it didn't require anything that was beyond what I knew myself to be capable of. It did not guarantee enlightenment. But my teachers told me that if I did the practice long enough it was almost inevitable.

Neither Tim McCarthy, my first Zen teacher, nor Gudo Nishijima, my second, was too fussed about whatever enlightenment experiences they'd had. I never heard any details of such things from either of them. And yet there was definitely something different about them. I could feel it when I was in their presence. And I knew they wouldn't lie to me. You can just tell that about some people.

There are two main schools of Zen, Soto and Rinzai. My teachers were both from the Soto tradition. I knew that the Rinzai tradition was much more focused on enlightenment. It is designed to foster these experiences and to test students on their levels of attainment. There is a series of training exercises called koans that are supposed to indicate deepening levels of understanding. In this system, the teachers ask you strange questions — koans — and you have to answer them.

Certain koans seem worth more enlightenment points than others. Koans such as "Does a dog have Buddha nature?" and "What is the sound of one hand clapping?" are freshman-level koans, while others, such as "All things return to the One, but where does the One return to?" and "What was the shape of your face before your parents were born?" are more like senior-level koans. I never followed this system myself, and I understand that not all Rinzai teachers do, either. But roughly speaking, this is how it is usually presented.

When I was in Nijmegen, the Netherlands, a few years ago I was introduced to a guy named Ton Lathouwers.* Ton is in his seventies but doesn't look it. He's slim and fit, and he assured me, "I do not paint my hair," even though his hair is still mostly jet black. He started his Buddhist career in the 1970s by studying Zen with Masao Abe (which is pronounced "ah-bay" and does not rhyme with *babe*), a famous author and professor of Buddhism who came to the West to try and stimulate dialogs between Buddhists and Christians. Ton said that Abe was in great distress during a Zen retreat and screamed at his teacher, "I cannot find any place to stand!" His teacher told him to stand right at that place where there is nowhere to stand. That's how Abe found God. Although Abe was not a Rinzai practitioner, his experience with this question is something like what happens in the less rigidly structured versions of koan practice.

I used to find the idea of koan study very attractive. At least you knew where you stood with a Rinzai teacher. In Soto it was all very vague. One teacher I spoke to told me that people in the Rinzai tradition almost always have some kind of enlightenment experience. But according to him usually their experiences are not very deep. On the other hand, he said, in the Soto tradition relatively few people have enlightenment experiences. But the ones who do tend to have really deep ones. How one measures such things I do not know.

As for my own incident, I haven't reread what I wrote about it in *Hardcore Zen*, so chances are I'll probably contradict some of what I said in that book. But the superficial facts are quite simple. One day, in the early autumn, I was walking to work. As I got to a little bridge that crossed over a very narrow part of the Sengawa River, I suddenly became open to everything in the universe throughout all of time.

I had crossed that bridge every day for years. It was my customary route to work. I would take the Odakyu train from Shinjuku station to Seijo Gakuen Mae station, get off there, walk by the KFC with the plastic statue of Colonel Sanders out front and down the street, make a turn

---

* That's not a typo. His name is Ton and not Tom.

at the river, walk along the river to the bridge, and cross over. Then I'd walk behind Toho Studios, where they made the Godzilla films. Sometimes I would be lucky enough, when I peeked in, to see them actually filming a guy in a Godzilla suit walking around in a miniature Pacific Ocean, complete with tiny battleships. After that I'd wind my way through the back streets to Tsuburaya Productions, the company I worked for.

The day I met God was completely normal, probably a Tuesday or some other nondescript weekday. One of the oddest things about what happened is that I cannot place a date on it. I suspect it was in the late 1990s. My sense of time was knocked for a loop so hard that it's impossible for me even to reconstruct events enough to figure out what the hell year it was with any more accuracy than that, let alone what day. That's very odd, even to me.

The reason I cannot fix a date on it is that the incident occurred outside of time. I know that sounds bizarre. But this was something Tim had told me about so-called enlightenment experiences. We usually think that everything happens at a specific point in time. Well, this didn't. And maybe nothing really does. But we'll leave that aside for now.

Although this happened to me, Brad, in a city called Tokyo on a certain day of the week in a specific year, the incident did not occur on a specific day in a specific location to anyone in particular. It occurred throughout time and everywhere in the universe. It did not happen only to me. It happened just as much to you.

To even say that it was an "incident" that "happened" does not do it justice. It was not an isolated event. It was and is the true condition of all things all the time. It was as much a living, breathing entity as you or I, maybe more so. It wasn't merely an incident that happened. It was also a presence that was, is, and always will be there. It underlies everything. It is the very basis of all experience. It was more me than I could ever be. But it was not me at all.

What I had assumed was me, a guy named Brad Warner who occupied a specific location, had a specific history, could do certain things and could not do other things, had a specific height, weight, and shoe size, this thing I called Brad Warner was, I saw, spread throughout the universe and throughout all of time.

This was God. Is God. Will always be God. I can't deny the experience any more than I could deny I have a nose. It wasn't Brad Warner at all. And yet Brad Warner couldn't possibly exist except as part of it. Nor could it — God — exist apart from Brad Warner. Or apart from you, for that matter.

After it happened there was no comedown, no sense that anything special had happened. Yes, it was extraordinary by definition. And yet it was absolutely ordinary. It was the very root of all experience, both ordinary and extraordinary, both mundane and exciting, both now and outside of now. For a short while I could see not only out of my own eyes but also through the eyes of God looking at me. But it was not a short while. It was forever.

And what you have just read is the cheapest, most tawdry piece of enlightenment porn ever written. Absolute crap. I'm not just making it up, mind you. It's all true. But even so, I have to warn you that you should not believe a word of it. I'm not kidding. You really shouldn't.

Some people call these experiences *kensho*, which means seeing into one's true nature. I once spoke to a Zen teacher who told me that she had only had one *kensho* experience but that it was enough. She didn't say this in a way that sounded like bragging, like she'd had the ultimate *kensho* and didn't need any more. She said it like you might say, "I ate fried worms once and once was enough." It was almost — but not quite — like she was glad it was over and she didn't want to have to go through it again. I can relate.

In a way it's similar to losing your virginity. You can be like Gene Simmons, the bass player from KISS, and have sex every day with a different partner for thirty or forty years. But you still lose your virginity only once. The sex you experience after that first time may be exciting, it may even be a whole lot better in some respects (or perhaps in all respects). But it's never the same because the element of surprise is gone forever.

It's the same with enlightenment. I've had other incidents since then. But they were never like that one. They never can be.

For a while after it happened, I kept wanting it to happen again. I would wonder if I was doing something wrong when it didn't happen again. I would wonder if God had granted me a moment in his presence and then gotten too busy to make time for me anymore. It made me sadder than you can possibly imagine.

This sense of longing led to other incidents that looked like what I thought an enlightenment experience ought to be. Instead, though, they were just my ego trying to grab onto the experience to prove that it was the biggest and baddest ego in the whole universe.

I also wrote about one of those later experiences in *Hardcore Zen*. If you've read the book it was in the part in which I found myself enlarging and enlarging until I engulfed all of creation. Some people have misread that and been really impressed. Nobody should be impressed by a story like that.

I am no more God than you, dear reader, are. The experience itself confers nothing of what we commonly think of as "godly qualities" on a person — though many like to claim it does. It does not give you an understanding of what happened any more than the experience of a car crash gives you an understanding of what caused the crash.

This is why I am so against schemes that claim to speed people along the enlightenment path as quickly as possible. To have such an experience when you're not grounded as a person is a very dangerous thing. You need to work through a lot of your personal shit before you get into something like this, or you'll only be able to experience it in terms of your own personal shit. You don't have to achieve full-scale Buddha-like serenity. But you do have to do some real work to get yourself a little more balanced if an experience like this is going to have any real value.

I suspect that some of our worst megalomaniacs and mass murderers may be people who had experiences like the one I had and misconstrued them in tragic ways. I also suspect that a lot of people confined to mental institutions and prisons had experiences like this and did not know how to deal with them. Plenty of people have claimed that I got way too big for my britches after it happened to me. And maybe they're right.

In and of themselves enlightenment experiences are not something to be envied or sought after. They are not necessarily ecstatic or blissful. In some sense they have aspects of ecstasy or bliss. But they're not all about good feelings. They cover the entire range of all possible feelings. And, if you're like me, the ego can even create a story based on the experience that makes you feel pretty bad.

But I came away from the experience knowing certain things for absolute fact. I know now that God exists. I know that I am not nearly so limited and small as I had supposed. I no longer fear death.

I have to qualify that last statement. I still don't want to die. I still don't want to get a terrible disease or get into some kind of awful accident. Last year when I was lecturing in Berlin I came down with some kind of weird fever. At the hospital the German doctors told me they were worried I might have meningitis. You'd better believe I was scared. I kept thinking, "Second-rate Buddhist author Brad Warner, who was never nearly as good as Deepak Chopra or Eckhart Tolle, died in Berlin of meningitis during a largely unsuccessful tour of Europe." That's just what I need as an obituary. "Warner was known mostly for going on the Internet and making fun of much more important Buddhist masters by using a sock monkey."*

So I do fear death in the sense that I find the prospect of dying pretty scary. But I no longer fear that I will one day be annihilated and

---

* Yes, you can find a video of me and a sock monkey on YouTube. That's all I'll say.

cease to exist. I can see now that the very idea is kind of absurd and meaningless. That doesn't mean I believe that I, Brad Warner, will live forever. But I understand that what I had thought of as me is not really small enough to have a beginning and end. I'll talk about this more in a later chapter.

Life is as much a fundamental component of the real universe as gravity and energy and matter. My life as Brad and the universe's life as the universe are fundamentally the same life. And your life and the universe's life are also the same. "Do not mistakenly assume," Dogen says, "that your self is only what you can see and know. What you cannot see and cannot know is also part of your self."

If my guesswork about the date is correct, it's been more than ten years since that day by the Sengawa River. What's left of the experience in my memory is like what's left of any experience. Memory fades. But more than that, memory is only the traces left in the brain by an experience. The brain doesn't record everything. It can't.

I felt it was necessary to write again about the experience because it may help put the rest of what I want to say about God into some kind of context. I am not speaking here just about my speculations regarding God or my thoughts regarding God. I am trying to talk also about my real experience of God.

You may want to ask me how I can know that experience was real and not a hallucination. You may want to challenge me to prove how what I'm saying here about this experience is different from some guy saying how when he was born again God told him to hate fags. I understand that. But I'm not really interested in pursuing those kinds of questions. I don't want to prove to anyone that my experience was real. It's not necessary or even possible. It won't make what happened any less real if you disbelieve or any more real if you believe it.

It's always a major turn-off to me when believers in God are obviously desperate to convince others. That kind of approach seems to stem from deep insecurity. It's as if they think that what they believe can only be true if everyone else is convinced.

As I've said, my Zen teachers never seemed eager to prove that they'd had some great awakening experience. And that's one of the reasons I started practicing and studying Zen. I got into it for a number of other reasons too, but the biggest one was that I wanted to know if God really existed. Even at a very young age I could see the rationality for deciding God was no more real than Santa Claus. And yet I felt there had to be something more to the world than could be accounted for by science and rationality. Existence itself is extraordinarily mysterious, no matter how you explain it. Why *is* there something rather than nothing?

Through a number of bizarre accidents of fate I ended up meeting a couple of Zen teachers. Neither of these people claimed to be special in any way. Yet they seemed to possess some kind of answer to this question. They did not claim their answer was unique to them. In fact, they said it was available to anyone who had the courage and patience to look for it.

The answer they had wasn't something they could tell me. It couldn't be put into words. And yet it was there. I remember getting very frustrated at a retreat with Nishijima Roshi and talking to him about it. I felt as if I was getting nowhere in my practice. I'd been at it for ten whole years by then, and nothing was clear at all. I threw up my hands and whined, "But I want to know where the stars and the sun and the entire universe come from!"

Nishijima just kind of smiled and said, "You can find out." As if it was the easiest thing in the world.

A few more years of hard effort later, one day, during a morning walk by the Sengawa River, I found out.

CHAPTER 6

TALKING TO ZEN MONKS ABOUT GOD

After the incident by the Sengawa River I didn't just drop my Zen practice, feeling that I'd accomplished what I'd wanted to and no longer needed it. In fact, I felt like I needed it more than ever. I've kept on sitting every day and attending retreats. I even started running some of my own retreats. After moving to California in 2004 I made friends with some of the folks up at the San Francisco Zen Center and thereby wormed my way into a loose association with one of the loveliest Zen places on Earth, the monastic retreat center Tassajara near Big Sur in Northern California. Every summer for the past few years I've spent a month there.

Tassajara is the most isolated place I've been to. Just to get there you have to travel up, up, up into the mountains and then down, down, down into a canyon along a fourteen-mile narrow dirt road with a steep cliff on one side and a dense forest on the other. TV, radio, and cell phone signals don't reach Tassajara, and naturally there's no Internet access. When you're in Tassajara you feel like the outside world is very far away.

I went to Tassajara my first summer ostensibly to do two different things. For most of the month I was down there, I was kind of a glorified waiter. For my last couple of days at Tassajara I was a guest lecturer, and I gave a talk titled "Dogen's Concept of God."

My friend Greg Fain is the *tanto*, or practice leader, at Tassajara. Greg invited me to come down and give some talks. I didn't just want to zip in there, say some stuff, and zip out. So I asked Greg if I could sign up to be a work practice student for a few weeks and then give some talks at the end of my stay. He conferred with the management, and they said I could do this crazy thing.

First, let me explain what a work practice student is. Tassajara wasn't always a Zen monastery. In the 1860s it was established as a resort. People went up and down that big, long road not for spiritual awakening but to booze it up and lounge around in the natural hot springs. I've heard there was even a brothel on the premises. In 1966 Tassajara was on its last legs as a vacation spot and the San Francisco Zen Center bought the place to use as a monastery, but the former owners stipulated they must keep the summer guest season going. These days the San Francisco Zen Center finances the monastery at Tassajara by opening it up as a resort every summer. For four months the Zen students are moved into the shabbier cabins, and the better cabins are rented to rich folks who want to hang out in the hot springs.

There is no paid staff at Tassajara. All the guest relations and suchlike are handled by work practice students. These students follow a regular Zen schedule in the mornings and evenings and spend the rest of their days doing the jobs necessary to keep the resort running. This includes cleaning rooms, making beds, cooking, keeping the pool and bathhouse running, keeping cranky customers happy, and so forth.

I'd been traveling around the world for three or four months before going to Tassajara. I was the toast of Europe, the Middle East, and Asia, with rabid fans clawing their way to see me in Helsinki, Belfast, Warsaw, Toulouse, Berlin, Amsterdam, Tel Aviv, Shizuoka, and elsewhere. Okay, so I'm exaggerating a bit. I'm not *really* that famous, though I have been stopped in the street by folks who like my books, and once, when I was paying by credit card for a used book in Knoxville, Tennessee, the clerk said, "I *thought* I recognized you! I love your books!" And although most of my tours have gone really well, a couple of personal appearances in Europe attracted as few as three people. Still, I am famous enough nowadays that it's starting to be a little weird. It's usually nice. But sometimes it's awkward.

My lifestyle was drawing me further and further away from my Zen practice. It's hard to sit zazen twice a day when you're zipping around from place to place faster than a speeding bullet, meeting people, hanging out, seeing the sights, getting fed, and all the rest. I felt that I needed the rigorous schedule, the ridiculous rules, and the hard work Tassajara requires of its students to get myself back on track.

I was assigned to the dining room, where I was something like a waiter or busboy. I served food, brewed and poured coffee, bused dishes, scraped compost into buckets, and did most of the stuff waiters or busboys do. I even opened wine bottles. It's BYOB there; no alcohol is sold or served, though it is sometimes poured. That was on days when I wasn't assigned to be a dishwasher.

I have to admit, my first few days on the job I was all like, "Don't these people know who I am? I am one of the most important voices in Buddhism today! Refill your coffee? Ha! You should be so lucky as to get your coffee refilled by a star of my caliber!"

Again, I'm exaggerating. Though I did sometimes feel a little resentful. And a few guests recognized me. But by and large the rich folks who rent rooms at Tassajara aren't my target audience. I was more often spotted by students. That was okay, though, because it doesn't take long getting over being star-struck by a guy you see hauling stinky buckets of compost and cleaning encrusted crud off the samovar.* As Greg said, when I told him about all this, "It's a great way to study the self." It sure was.

I had a few adventures and met some amazing people. I formed a punk rock band and got my first Mohawk (which looked great with my hated Zen robes, which I wore every day). I learned some new jokes

---

* A samovar, by the way, is a big machine for making industrial-sized quantities of coffee. I learned useful stuff while I was there!

(Q: What has two knees and swims in the ocean? A: A two-knee fish!).
It was totally worth it, which is why I went back the next two summers
for more of the same.

But I also had to talk about Dogen and God. Twice a week they
have what they call Dining Room Talks. They clear out the dining
room between lunch and dinner and someone gives a speech. Sometimes it's a guest from the outside world, and sometimes it's someone
who lives at Tassajara. I will try to encapsulate here what I said.

People often think of Buddhism, particularly Zen Buddhism, as a
religion without God. Remember, D. T. Suzuki, whose works are still
considered authoritative by many, said "Zen has no God to worship,
no ceremonial rites to observe, no future abode to which the dead are
destined." Furthermore he said, "last of all, Zen has no soul whose wel-
fare is to be looked after by somebody else and whose immortality is a
matter of intense concern with some people."

Dogen would probably agree with this. Dogen wrote a volumi-
nous treatise on Zen practice called *Shobogenzo*, or "Treasury of the
True Dharma Eye," which I mentioned earlier, as well as numerous
other works on Zen. He also brought the Soto school of Zen Buddhism
from China to Japan. In Japan, Soto soon became the most popular
school of Zen Buddhism and remains so today.

What makes Dogen different from most philosophers is that it
wasn't just talk with him. He had a practice. Dogen advocated a type of
meditation he called *shikantaza*, or "just sitting." This type of meditation is goal-less. It's not focused on attaining special states of mind or
insight, and it's unconcerned with the so-called enlightenment experiences that some other schools of Buddhism consider essential to the
practice. Dogen taught that sitting zazen, which means "seated meditation," itself is enlightenment. To Dogen, the sitting was everything.

I've been talking a lot about *shikantaza* in this book, without actually naming it as such, because it's the practice I do every day. After
nearly thirty years of daily *shikantaza* I have yet to get to the bottom of

it. Ironically, even though it's taken so many years to get even a little way into this practice, I can state the philosophical basis for it quite simply.

Shikantaza proceeds from the view that all our thoughts and perceptions are by necessity incomplete and, to either a large or small degree, mistaken. There is no way to encompass reality in your mind. The brain does its job, in part, by deliberately ignoring most of the data it receives and by focusing only on the material it needs. Furthermore, the data the brain receives is itself already limited to what our senses are able to perceive.

One of the things the brain does is create an image of the self. Like all its images, the image of the self is by necessity incomplete. But it's a model that is usually useful for most of the activities we engage in.

The problem is that we believe that these various incomplete and mistaken images our brain has created — including the image of our self — are reality. We think we are perceiving and conceiving of reality when, in fact, reality is beyond our perceptive ability and our powers of conception. At the same time, however, we are living in reality. The fact that we cannot grasp the totality of what we're living in doesn't change this.

Shikantaza-style meditation practice forces us to fully live in reality as it is beyond our conceptions and perceptions. It forces us to remain profoundly in the here and now, even when our minds, and often our senses too, try to seduce us with beautiful or frightening images of other places and times or to convince us that sitting and staring at a wall is really dull and that there must be better things going on elsewhere.

As one might expect from a monk devoted to this style of meditation, Dogen's writing never mentions God specifically. The monotheism of Judaism, Christianity, and Islam was completely unknown to him.

In spite of this, I believe that Dogen's Buddhism directly addresses questions about the nature of God and about our relationship to God. One chapter of *Shobogenzo* in particular presents us with a clear description of Dogen's concept of God.

The chapter is called *"Inmo"* in Japanese. In the introduction to the translation of this chapter he did with Mike Cross, Gudo Nishijima explains the word *inmo*: "*Inmo* is a colloquial word in Chinese, meaning 'it,' 'that,' or 'what.' We usually use the words 'it,' 'that,' or 'what' to indicate something we do not need to explain. Therefore Buddhist philosophers in China used the word *inmo* to suggest something ineffable. At the same time, one of the aims of studying Buddhism is to realize reality, and according to Buddhist philosophy, reality is something ineffable. So the word *inmo* was used to indicate the truth, or reality, which in Buddhist philosophy is originally ineffable."

Whenever I read this chapter I tend to substitute the word *God* for *inmo*. I don't know what else Dogen could possibly be talking about other than God.

All words are misleading. This fact is one of the cornerstones of Zen philosophy. There is no way to choose exactly the right word or phrase to fully encompass and clearly communicate any thought. As Lou Reed rightly points out in the song "Some Kinda Love," "between thought and expression lies a lifetime." Even thoughts themselves are incomplete. So language is at best an approximation of an approximation.

Still, it's useful to look at what Dogen wrote about his concept of God. So here goes.

In the chapter Dogen begins by quoting an ancient Zen teacher who said, "If you want to attain the matter that is it [*inmo*], you must be a person who is it [*inmo*]. Already being a person who is it [*inmo*], why worry about the matter that is it [*inmo*]?" This statement reflects Dogen's original reasons for pursuing Buddhist practice. He had heard from various teachers that Buddhism's message was that we were already innately perfect just as we were. Then why, he asked, do we need to perform the various rituals and practices of Buddhism, such as meditation? No one he met was able to answer his question, until he traveled to China, where he met Master Tendo Nyojo,* who told him that the practice of zazen was enlightenment itself.

---

* In Chinese, Tiantong Rujing.

In the next paragraph Dogen begins to describe what this "it" is, and this is where he starts to talk about God. He says that another name for "it" is the "supreme truth of *bodhi.*" The word *bodhi* means "enlightenment" or "awakening." Dogen says, "The situation of this supreme truth of *bodhi* is such that even the whole universe in ten directions is just a small part of the supreme truth of *bodhi*: it may be that the truth of *bodhi* abounds beyond the universe."

To my way of thinking this is just another way of describing God. Of course, this is not the personal creator God revered by lots of religious people. In her book *A History of God*, Karen Armstrong quotes the Roman Catholic catechism she had to memorize as a child, which said, "God is the Supreme Spirit, Who alone exists of Himself and is infinite in all perfections." Dogen is clearly not talking about this kind of God.

The problem with the idea of God as an infinite being is that we're already contradicting ourselves. Something that's infinite is unlimited. But the word *being*, when used as a noun, refers to one being among other beings. God can't possibly be infinite unless he is also not infinite. I suppose the catechism gives itself an out by describing God as "infinite *in all perfections*" rather than truly infinite.

But Dogen's "it" doesn't indicate a God who sits on a throne in heaven being perfect and infinite and who is forever separate from the universe he created. When you really examine it, all the attributes commonly ascribed to God ultimately make no sense. Everybody knows the old joke, "Can God make a rock so heavy even he can't lift it?" It sounds kind of juvenile, but it's actually a very good question that points out the absurdity of limiting God in any way, including by saying he is infinite as opposed to things that are not infinite. One of my favorite parts of Dogen's chapter about God addresses this matter:

Already we possess the real features of a "person who is it"; we should not worry about the already-present "matter that is it." Even worry itself is just "the matter that is it," and so it is beyond worry. This state cannot be fathomed even by the consideration of buddha and it cannot be fathomed by the consideration of the whole universe. It can only be described "Already you are a person who is it: why worry about [attaining] the matter that is it?"

To me this is the perfect description of the infinite, of God. But it's not an intellectual supposition about what infinity might be like. It's more a description of one man's deep and very human connection with the infinite. This connection is not unique to Dogen. We all have it.

We don't need to search for God or wonder whether God exists. Our very sense of wonder is God wondering. This is more than an intellectual assurance of God's presence, or some clever twisting of words. Dogen was writing about his real experience.

Dogen goes on to say, about God's interaction with the universe and with us, "We ourselves are tools that 'it' possesses within this universe in ten directions." In other words, God is not remote and removed from our everyday experience. We ourselves are the means by which God experiences his creation, which is also himself.

We may doubt that this is so. But, Dogen says, "We know it is so because the body and the mind both appear in the universe, yet neither is our self." To illustrate this point he says, "The body, already, is not 'I.' Its life moves on through days and months, and we cannot stop it even for an instant. Where have the red faces [of our youth] gone? When we look for them, they have vanished without a trace. When we reflect carefully, there are many things in the past that we will never meet again."

Most modern Western philosophy argues a belief in the ultimate separation of body and mind, or matter and spirit. We are told that we must side either with the materialists, who insist that we are just this body, or with spiritual people, who say that we are just a mind, or a soul, that resides within the body. Even most Eastern religions insist on the same idea.

But Buddhism rejects this premise entirely. The Heart Sutra, which is the core text of Zen Buddhism, says, "Form is emptiness, emptiness is form." There is no division between body (form) and spirit (emptiness) or between matter and mind. The division we think we perceive and experience is just one of the many categories into which the brain divides our real experience.

I suspect that the body-mind division may be the ultimate division created by the brain. It appears to be a boundary line that our brains are designed not to cross. There may be a very good reason we are wired this way.

Human beings have the biggest, most powerful brains we know of. Our cleverness has been our main survival tool. We can imagine stuff and transform that imagined stuff into real things. We can imagine a spear and imagine stabbing a marauding stegosaurus* with that spear, then go build that spear and live to produce descendants.

But in order to do this we have to understand very clearly the difference between the stuff of our imaginations (one of the definitions of emptiness) and the physical stuff of the real world (form). We need to be able to do this even when the stuff of our imaginations becomes so detailed it's almost tangible. I believe our brains may have been honed by evolution to make a very sharp distinction between the real and the imagined. Those among our ancestors who couldn't differentiate between the things they thought about and the things they actually encountered were doomed.

Although we see body and mind as eternally separate, in our real experience body and mind always function together. This is even true in our dreams. I'm sure you've had the experience of dreaming about large bodies of water, then waking up to discover you have to pee really bad. The body asserts itself even in states we tend to think of as purely mental, just as the mind asserts itself in states we conceive of as purely physical.

---

* I know that the stegosaurus was extinct 100 million years before the first humans appeared. But I always loved those movies where cavemen fight dinosaurs.

Dogen tells us, "Although the state of sincerity does exist, it is not something that lingers in the vicinity of the personal self." It's far too cool to hang out with the likes of you! This "state of sincerity" is one of the more difficult concepts Dogen raises. My first Zen teacher used to talk a lot about sincerity, and I was always confused about what he meant.

.Sincerity in this case is not just honesty. It's something deeper than that. The word is used to indicate a state that is completely open and unaffected. It is us, as we truly are, without any attempt to disguise ourselves, even in the ways we usually disguise ourselves to ourselves.

The word that Nishijima and Cross have translated as "sincere mind" is sekishin, which literally means "red mind." The color red indicates rawness, like a piece of uncooked meat. So it refers to something untainted or pure, something as it exists in its natural state before we make any deliberate changes to it.

This sincere state does not linger in the vicinity of the personal self. You are not what you imagine yourself to be. That imagined "self" is just another concept the brain creates to sort things out. The boundaries it posits for this thing it calls self don't really exist any more than any of the other boundaries the brain creates in order to make conceptual sense of the universe.

Even if the sincere mind is not the same as the personal sense of self, "there is something that, in the limitlessness, establishes the [bodhi] mind." The bodhi mind is the will toward the truth. Our longing for the truth is the truth itself. We are always at least dimly aware that we live better when we live in accordance with what is true. All the religions I know about say this. The problem is that most religions proceed to try and explain the truth and then insist that we agree with their explanation. In Buddhism we're not very concerned with explanations of the truth. We're interested in living it.

According to Dogen, we live the truth when, "abandoning our former playthings we hope to hear what we have not heard before and we seek to experience what we have not experienced before." In other words, that which we have never heard or experienced before is the present moment. This moment is, by definition, something you have never experienced. Even if you've stood in a dozen subways reading countless books before, you've never stood in *this* subway on *this* day reading *this* book ever before. The things we have heard and experienced before include our received wisdom, our history, our preconceived notions. Most people remain rooted in the things they have experienced before. Even new experiences are quickly cataloged and referenced to the past.

Yet Dogen says that this is not entirely of our own doing. We arouse this *bodhi*-mind because we are people who are "it." But if you're skeptical about God, this idea might strike you as something akin to saying, "I know God exists because I believe in God and only God could make me believe in God." This, of course, is circular logic. It's not really defensible. But this is emphatically not what Dogen is saying here.

Rather, he is pointing at something that is beyond matters of thought or belief. The very fact that we are here to ask questions about God is evidence that God exists. Or to put it another way, it is evidence that some kind of intelligence is at work in the universe. This intelligence is not far away *out there*. It is the very intelligence that makes it possible for you to comprehend this book. And I don't believe that intelligence is something produced by me alone for me alone. I think it's something that what I call "me" partakes of in much the same way I partake of air or sunlight. Some might try to say that God is pure consciousness. But that's not the Buddhist view, either. God is beyond consciousness and beyond unconsciousness. I'll talk more about this in a later chapter.

That's what I think Dogen believed about God. Because God is ultimately unknowable, Dogen made no effort to describe God's characteristics. God is just "it."

CHAPTER 7

WHY CALL IT BUDDHISM?

Nishijima Roshi always insisted that "Buddhism is just realism." He believed that if any idea in Buddhism could be proven wrong when judged against what is demonstrably true, then we ought to throw that idea away. Dogen would have agreed. But why call it "Buddhism" at all if it's just realism? I've thought about that a lot, and I'd like to leave God aside for a while and talk about it.

I was invited to Frankfurt, Germany, to lead a three-day sesshin, or retreat, by Regina Obendorfer, who is another student of Nishijima Roshi. The retreat was to be held in the Pagoda Phat Hue (Buddhist Wisdom Pagoda). It was once a carpet factory, and it looks like it. But the Vietnamese monks who bought the place did a good job converting it into a working Zen monastery. Rumors surfaced much later that the temple was involved in some sort of scandal. But I never found out what it was. In any case, we just rented the place.

Vietnamese Zen is very different from Japanese Zen. The two traditions split off from each other several hundred years ago, though accounts differ as to when exactly the split occurred. And the two cultures are quite different in their approach to life. The Japanese are reserved and tend to prefer understated building and room designs. Their temples are often even more understated than their houses. The

Vietnamese, on the other hand, are much more expressive people over-all, and their temples reflect this.

I had never been in a Zen temple with so much red and gold and purple and other bright colors everywhere. Temples in Japan may be big and imposing, but inside they are generally full of earth tones, with maybe a bit of red accenting. The main halls in Japan are usually elabo-rately decorated and sometimes a bit gaudy. But even most of the main halls I've seen in Japan were somber by comparison to any part of the Frankfurt pagoda. I wasn't sure how the style of Zen I taught was going to work in a place like this.

In the morning, the monks who lived in the temple had their medi-tation practice, which I figured we'd just incorporate into our schedule. But their style of morning meditation was also quite different from any I'd ever experienced.

Morning zazen meditation in a Japanese temple starts off very loudly with a clanging wake-up bell, but things quiet way down right away. After you scramble to put on your clothes, brush your teeth, and run to the meditation hall, there's a much quieter bell to start zazen. Then you sit for at least a half hour but usually longer in com-plete silence, after which there may or may not be a time of chanting and ritual bows. In keeping with the austerity of Zen, the chanting is done in a monotone. At Nishijima's sesshins the ceremonial aspects were even more muted than usual. At his retreats the leader comes in very quietly, silently offers incense to the Buddha statue at the center of the meditation room, and does three prostrations. And there's no chanting.

At the pagoda, they sang a song every morning. Much of the song was in a foreign language. It might have been Vietnamese. But I suspect it was something more ancient, like Sanskrit. A few English phrases were interspersed. I remember hearing "shining in all directions" and "bring your mind to meditation." The chant ended with the repeated refrain "namu Shakyamuni Buddha," a Sanskrit intonation meaning "hail to Shakyamuni Buddha."

Bells were rung; incense and candles were lit. There was some business that I didn't quite understand involving putting fruit out on the altar. It was lovely. Then the Vietnamese monks settled down and did their silent meditation for about half an hour. After that they left. They were not on retreat and probably had jobs to go to. The participants of my retreat continued sitting, facing the walls for the rest of the day.

All these differences raise the question, What does it mean to be a Buddhist? Even though the two groups in the pagoda that weekend were not only both Buddhist but Zen Buddhist, they were quite different from each other. And anyway, why even call yourself a Buddhist at all? If it's just realism as Nishijima said, why does it need any other name than that?

I've been struggling for years to answer that question. My first Zen teacher once said that he generally didn't call himself a Buddhist. He said that if someone held a gun to his head and said, "State your religious affiliation, or I'll kill you," he'd say he was a Buddhist. But otherwise he didn't bother.

I take basically the same view. Unfortunately I've kind of outed myself as a Buddhist by writing books on the subject. In many of the circumstances I find myself in it's impossible to deny that I'm a Buddhist, so I don't. But when I meet people in random places that have nothing to do with my work as an author or as a monk, I usually don't tell them I'm a Buddhist.

In fact, even though I've written books about it, I don't feel like I'm any great expert on Buddhism in the way people usually define the term. I am not a scholar. Outside the works of Dogen, I don't read a whole lot of books on Buddhism. Frankly, most of them bore me. And even when it comes to Dogen, my scholarship is hardly first-rate. Dogen wrote a lot of material, and much of it I am only passingly familiar with or have not read at all. What little understanding and insight I have comes from Buddhist practice. It is through zazen practice and face-to-face interaction with my Buddhist teachers that I have gained whatever knowledge I have of Buddhism. The scholarly side of Buddhism seems totally removed from that. It's hard to even see the relationship between the two sometimes. In fact, many of our greatest Buddhist scholars do not practice any form of meditation at all. Scholarship and practice are very different things.

Another reason I don't tell people I'm a Buddhist is that, as I've stated, I'm not interested in converting people. Obviously, I like to tell people about Buddhist philosophy and practice because I think it's interesting and useful. Also, there's a lot of misinformation out there on the subject of Buddhism. As Buddhism becomes trendier, the number of scams based on misunderstandings or plain old willful distortions of Buddhist ideas are on the increase.

But back to the key question. Why be Buddhist at all?

I don't even like the word *Buddhism*, which was created by nineteenth-century European investigators of Eastern religions. At first they believed they had discovered a religion that worshipped a God named Buddha in much the same way that Christians, Muslims, and Jews worshipped Jehovah. Because Buddha statues showed a guy with curly hair and thick lips, some scholars speculated this Buddha fellow may have originally been an African god.

There are a couple of very good books on the subject of how Westerners came to understand Buddhism, particularly *The British Discovery of Buddhism* by Philip C. Almond and *The Search for Buddha* by Charles Allen. The first appearance of the word *Buddhism* can be traced back to a British author in 1801. There is no evidence that any of the people we now refer to as Buddhists used anything like that term even in their own languages. Dogen, for example, uses the word *bukkyo*, which is often translated as "Buddhism" but means something more like "Buddha's teaching," which is a different thing. The word *Buddhism* implies that Buddhists are members of one of the great religions of the world, which are usually counted to include Christianity, Islam, Judaism, Hinduism, Taoism, and Buddhism. These are all considered to be different flavors of the same basic thing. You can score points with certain types of people by saying you think each religion is equally valid. This idea can also get you votes if you're a politician, and can sell you some books if you're a writer. People love to hear it. But nobody really believes it.

Many question whether Buddhism belongs on this list at all. Some argue that it isn't a religion but a philosophy. I'm not sure it fits into the category of philosophy any better than it does into the category of religion. Like most religions, Buddhism has specific rituals, and it has monks and priests who go through a process much like the ordination processes that exist in the great religions. These monks commonly dress in a specific uniform and generally sport the same haircut. That isn't much like any school of philosophy I'm aware of.

The place where Buddhism really differs from other religions is in its attitude toward the material world. All the other great religions are spiritual. Buddhism says that both the material aspects of reality and the spiritual aspects of reality are manifestations of something that transcends classification as either spiritual or material. So what's it mean to be a Buddhist?

Someone once asked me in an interview, "How do I become a Buddhist?" I found the question a bit funny because even to ask such a question of me already supposes that I want other people to become Buddhists. As I said, as far as I'm concerned it's not really very important if you do or you don't.

However, in the Zen school there is a straightforward answer to the question of how one becomes a Buddhist. Wonder of wonders! A straightforward answer in Zen! The process is simple. You undergo a ceremony called *jukai* in which you take a public vow to abide by the ten precepts of Buddhism. These precepts are 1) Don't kill, 2) Don't steal, 3) Don't misuse sexuality, 4) Don't lie, 5) Don't cloud the mind with intoxicants, 6) Don't speak of others' errors or faults, 7) Don't praise yourself and berate others, 8) Don't be covetous, 9) Don't give way to anger, and 10) Don't defile Buddha, the Buddhist teachings, or the Buddhist community.

After you publicly declare that you will follow these precepts for the rest of your life, you do a few little dance steps and then your teacher waves some incense around, gives you a special Buddhist name and maybe a piece of colored cloth to hang around your neck, and then you are officially a Buddhist. The whole thing takes about half an hour. Some places make you do a lot of preparatory work for the ceremony. Some places only require that you show up.

Some might feel they can't uphold the precepts unless they take a public vow to do so. But I don't feel like I uphold the precepts any better after having publicly vowed to do so* than I did before I took those vows. Many people have complained that I break precept number six regularly when I dare to criticize those who I believe misrepresent Buddhism. The same folks often also feel that I break number seven, the one about praising oneself, all the time. They think that when I criticize some of these rip-offs I am, in doing so, implying that I am some kind of genius Buddhist.

In fact, as I said, I don't feel that I'm any sort of genius Buddhist. It is precisely for this reason that it bugs me so much to see Buddhism so terribly misrepresented. When I see someone with a genuine Buddhist ordination doing things that even I can see directly contravene the most basic principles of Buddhism, it's shocking. I feel like a third grader watching a famous physics professor mess up an addition problem, and then seeing everyone accept what he said just because of the professor's reputation.

In the end I use the word *Buddhist* to describe myself by default. It's the easiest way to indicate the practice I do and the specific category of understanding I have about the way things are. To me Buddhism is not a religion or a philosophy. It's a practice and it's an attitude. It's

* I did so on three occasions — once with my teacher, once as part of my wedding ceremony (I'm divorced now, but the vows still hold), and once officially with the Soto-shu organization of Japan.

something you do (meditation) that produces a radically different out-look on life in general. This outlook affects everything you do. As an attitude it does not have a specific set of beliefs that have to be agreed on and adhered to. And yet when you recognize others who have the same attitude you know it almost instantly even when their beliefs differ from yours. It's kinda weird that way.

Buddhism is an unfortunate word for this practice, since it tends to divide me from others and to indicate a sectarian involvement and the belief that my sect can beat up other people's sects. But so does the word *American*, so does the word *vegetarian*, so does the word *male*, and so on.

As they say in Japan, *sho ga nai*. It can't be helped. So I'm a Buddhist. So what?

CHAPTER 8

MEDITATION IS THE PRACTICE OF DEATH

Maybe you're asking yourself why I'm so fired up about zazen and why I think doing it is more important than reading a truckload of books about Buddhism. I do it because meditation is the practice of death. I touched on the fear of death in an earlier chapter; let's talk about it some more here.

A guy named Eric sent me an email that went like this:

> While you've talked about death in all your books I can only remember your mentioning the fear of death once, and it was to say, in effect: Buddhism can't do anything about our fear of death. And wouldn't life kind of suck without it, anyway? I disagree. If I could live the rest of my life without the bone-chilling fear of nonexistence then I would be *much* happier.
>
> When I read that, I supposed you were referring to the biological fear hard-wired into us by evolution that makes most of us avoid things like playing chicken with trains and drinking Drano. If that's what you mean I totally agree. But what about the more existential fear that arises upon the contemplation of our death? When I squarely face the fact that my awareness will be annihilated in just a few short decades, it is enough to 1) keep me from sleeping and 2) make me really depressed.

I know that Buddhism says we die all the time. I know that there is no essential self that coheres through the years of a person's life. But it is still scary as hell to contemplate nothingness. So does zazen remedy that? If it does, great. But if it doesn't, then why do zazen as opposed to obliterating yourself with video games, wild sex, and booze? Saying the practice is its own reward is fine and dandy, but if it is still going to leave us blanched with terror and sadness at the omnipresence of death, then what's the point?

Zazen will not necessarily rid you of your fear of death. But lots of other things, such as booze, wild sex, and video games, definitely won't. They may distract you from your fear for a time. But eventually the fear catches up with you.

Like Eric, at one time I was absolutely terrified of death. When I was a teenager I realized that a horrifying illness (Huntington's disease) that often crippled and/or killed people before they reached the age that I am now ran in our family. My mom died from it in 2007, and two of my aunts died from it before that. I didn't think I had long to live, and I was scared shitless. Not many people are as lucky as I was to have to face death at such an early age. I'll get back to that in a bit.

When I looked into religions I felt like they were all about escaping from life. They offered ways to escape into a life in heaven or in Krishna Loka or a variety of other places. They didn't deny death — they were obsessed with it. But they did deny life. What they said translated to me as something like, "Trade your life now for a chance at something amazing after you die."

And they tried to make the trade sound reasonable. You only get to live in this world for a few decades. But the afterlife, they said, is eternal. So I was supposed to live a bland, boring, restricted life in the hopes of being rewarded for my perseverance and austerity with a really superterrific future in the afterlife that would last forever.

The problem with that was that I couldn't believe in the afterlife.

The evidence for its existence was just not convincing. Nor could I believe that God would put a lot of fun stuff in the world and then tell us to avoid it.

I knew I was living *this* life. So my quest became about how to make this life better. Some turn to hedonistic pleasures as a way to make this life better. That idea didn't work for me, either, for much the same reasons that the religious one failed for me. There isn't a lot of evidence that money, power, sex, and all that really lead to happiness. It's almost as irrational to believe in that as it is to believe in life after death. I was already well aware of the excessive lives of wealthy people like Elvis Presley and Howard Hughes, who had all they could possibly want and were still miserable.

Later there was Kurt Cobain, who did exactly what I'd been hoping I could do. I released a bunch of indie-label alt-rock albums in the 1980s, hoping that one day I'd get on the cover of some rock magazine like *Spin* or at least *Alternative Press*. I failed. But Cobain succeeded. He parlayed a shitty-paying career as an indie rocker into superstardom. Yet it made him suicidally depressed. This was a big shock because a life like his was precisely what I'd believed would lift me out of my own depression. I had always been a very pessimistic kid.

Then I started working in the movie industry. I routinely associated with famous people who were absolutely loaded with cash, and I saw that they were just as unhappy as the people who were struggling to make ends meet. I met people who had lots of fame and lots of money who exhausted themselves letting other people know they had lots of fame and lots of money.

On the other hand, Zen practice was all about how to make this life better, without offering any magic solutions. This was appealing because I didn't believe in magic solutions. Zen never got into questions of the afterlife. It demanded a moderate degree of austerity, not because you were trading austerity today for a future of wonders in paradise after you were dead, but because chasing after money, fame, sex, material goods, and power just added unnecessary stress to your life. And you wouldn't be satisfied even when you got those things. The austerity demanded by Zen practice was supposed to help you see the beauty in your own supposedly miserable existence. And for me it did. The most mundane things became inexplicably wondrous. What did I need to get rich for?

But then if we can't escape into orgies or drugs or buying stuff, how do we handle our fear of death? What about the fear of future oblivion?

The problem isn't so much death itself as it is the *fear* of death. I came to understand this fear better through my practice. I began to see that the root of this fear was a projection of my imaginary self into an imaginary future. I saw that it was a fear of things that were not real and never become real.

This doesn't exactly erase the fear of death. When I think about the possibility of Brad Warner disappearing forever, I don't really like it. As a matter of fact, I hate the idea. But I also understand that the fear this idea provokes is completely unreasonable.

What I'm about to say might seem like mysticism, but here goes anyhow. Once you start seeing this moment for what it really is, you understand that you can never actually be annihilated in the ways you previously imagined. What I think of as Brad Warner is a construct in my mind. It isn't real.

Yet that mental construct called Brad Warner is based on something real. This something can't really die because it was never really born, at least not in the sense we commonly think of things being born and dying. Yes, Brad Warner was born, and yes, Brad Warner will die. And yet he is not just an individual entity. He is also a temporary manifestation of something vast and unknowable that has no beginning and no end. The same goes for you.

Shunryu Suzuki, when he was dying of cancer, told his friend Dainin Katagiri, "I don't want to die." Katagiri replied, "Thank you for your great effort." They were both famous Zen masters. Why would a person who has transcended death say he didn't want to die?

I've heard that this statement freaked out a lot of Suzuki's followers. It implied either 1) that an enlightened master still fears death or
2) that their master was not actually enlightened because an enlightened master couldn't possibly fear death. Neither idea was very attractive to those who had put their faith in a master they thought would
deliver them from their fear of death.

But I don't think Suzuki's statement implies a fear of death, at least
not in the way most of us think of it. It implies that the teacher would
rather have lived longer. That's not really the same thing. I take that
statement to be almost an apology. A lot of people depended on Suzuki,
and he knew that he was letting them down by dying and leaving so
many important things unfinished. And maybe he also just didn't want
to die. Which is pretty reasonable, if you ask me. I don't want to die,
either. No sensible person does.

I used to lose sleep over my fear of death. Nowadays for me death
is about as scary as, say, the idea of a root canal. It's something I don't
want to go through, and if you gave me the option of avoiding death
altogether I'd definitely consider it. But the fear of death doesn't keep
me awake nights.

You have to understand, though, that however much I have overcome my fear of death I owe to years of often difficult practice. You
don't overcome this overwhelming fear by simply deciding you don't
want to be afraid of death or by rationalizing it away. It's not that easy.
If it was, everyone would do it.

The following is sure to ensure that this book will not sell nearly
as well as it could if I were smart enough to leave it out. But I can't. So
here goes. In order to deal with the fear of annihilation you have to face
annihilation again and again and again. It's not enough just to understand this intellectually. It's not enough just to read about this. You
need to watch yourself being annihilated *right now*. If you can man-
age to sit quietly as you disappear from existence moment by moment,
then you can see it's really nothing to be afraid of. You gotta meditate.
Nobody likes to hear that. But it's true.

One of my favorite stoner rock bands, Om, has a song called "Meditation Is the Practice of Death." It's an interesting phrase. It sounds sort of morbid. Or else it sounds like it's implying that meditation prepares one for death the way practicing bass prepares one for playing bass onstage.

But there's another way to interpret that phrase that neither sounds morbid nor implies that we are preparing ourselves for something that will occur in the future. Meditation is how we practice death as it occurs in the midst of life. It's how we see for ourselves our own annihilation and what it really means. It's how we learn that annihilation isn't some scary thing that happens at the end of life. Annihilation occurs all the time, faster than we can even be aware of it.

We imagine that we are a single being and that we exist across a series of moments. But that's not really what happens. There is no real difference between the moment in which we exist and we who exist within it. "Each moment is the universe," is how Katagiri said it. It makes no sense to fear annihilation when we experience it every moment. Annihilation is nothing to fear. Annihilation is the meaning of life.

When I have tried to understand exactly why I fear death it usually comes down to fearing the eternal loss of consciousness. Many people would define life and consciousness as very much the same thing. A lot of these people postulate that there is some kind of entity called consciousness that lives inside our material bodies, which they tend to think of as being nonconscious. This entity goes by a number of names. Christians call it the soul. Hindus call it *atman*.

Buddhism is famous for the teaching of *anatman*, usually translated as "no soul." Human beings are not a soul trapped inside a body but rather are the coming together of five *skandhas*. The word *skandha* means "heap."

One of the finest and most concise explanations I'm aware of regarding *skandhas* comes not from any ancient Buddhist text but from the singer Robyn Hitchcock, who as far as I know never actually studied Buddhism. In describing the genesis of his song "When I Was Dead" in a CD sent out to publicize his 1993 album *Respect*, he says,

> Given the existence of the universe, all the molecules in it have been here for billennia or something. They just keep juggling around. So you've got three of Shakespeare's molecules and you've got two of Himmler's or whatever it is. Part of your fingernail was part of St. Joseph of Arimathea's frontal lobe or something. Large parts of you were once a daffodil in Nova Scotia or something. You know, your feet used to be Winston Churchill. The same things keep getting recycled. It could be that when we pass away our psyches dissolve into lots of sort of strips of feeling. All the things that comprised us that were held together by our bodies dissolve. Hence [the line in the song] "I wasn't me to speak of just a thousand ancient feelings." Feelings that have been around since the beginning of human time.

The five heaps that make up a human being are usually reckoned to be form, feelings, perceptions, impulses, and consciousness. There are other translations of the words, but they're all fairly similar. It doesn't really matter what the particular heaps are. The divisions are largely arbitrary. They all bleed into one another.

Western religions and Hinduism tend to deal with only the first and last of these. Form is our material body, while consciousness is consciousness. As I've already said, most of our philosophies demand that we take sides, that we accept either form or consciousness as the true basis of our existence. But Buddhism sees both of these as mere constituents of what we are, along with three other things we rarely even take account of that are, they say, equally as important as form and consciousness.

Since consciousness is so crucial to the discussion of death and God we might well ask what the hell it is. We usually define life in terms of consciousness and death as its absence. Some people think that God is pure consciousness. Like Deepak Chopra, for example.

I know this because I have a Twitter account. I kind of hate it. I don't really understand what Twitter is supposed to be. I know it lets you write messages that are limited to 140 characters. I just don't understand who would want to post such things or read them — people with short attention spans who want to shorten them even further, I guess.

But I keep the account because it's useful. When I'm doing a live appearance somewhere I mention it on Twitter, and sometimes people who've seen it there show up. I also keep it because *Huffington Post* named me one of the top twelve Buddhists to follow on Twitter.*

I don't know why I chose to subscribe to Deepak Chopra's Twitter feed, but I did. Chopra is far from the worst of the money-spinning guru types out there. He strikes me as a reasonably sincere guy who knows how to charm an audience and has parlayed that charm into bazillions upon bazillions of dollars. There are times, I'll admit, that I wish I knew how to do that. But I think I'm far too curmudgeonly to ever get very popular. Deepak is not nearly as deep and profound as his fans think he is. But whatever. Neither was Kurt Cobain.

Anyway, I figured that Deepak, like pretty much all the other people on the spiritual megastar circuit who have Twitter feeds, didn't write his own tweets but had unpaid interns who scoured his books for pithy quotes to put up.† So one day I saw something on Deepak's Twitter feed that I wanted to respond to. It was this:

DEEPAK CHOPRA: Photons are invisible and colorless. The light of awareness makes them bright and colorful. Our consciousness creates the world.

So I responded as follows:

---

* I'm number ten. The fact that there are twelve Buddhists on Twitter is in itself kind of weird, if you ask me. And by the way, thank you, *Huffington Post*, for including me. I'm making jokes about it here, but it really is an honor.

† I write all my own, by the way. I can't even afford unpaid interns!

BRAD WARNER: @DeepakChopra Oh, Deepak. The world creates our consciousness too. You keep forgetting that!

Much to my amazement, Deepak himself tweeted me back!

DEEPAK CHOPRA: @BradWarner Consciousness is fundamental! The world exists only in consciousness, as does our mind and body.

BRAD WARNER: @DeepakChopra And consciousness only exists in the world, as does our body and mind.

DEEPAK CHOPRA: @BradWarner We are the makers of reality.

BRAD WARNER: @DeepakChopra And reality is the maker of us. Don't be so one-sided.

DEEPAK CHOPRA: @BradWarner The world is Maya (illusion). We are each other's fantasy.

At this point I told Deepak that he'd finally said something I agreed with, and it ended there.

If asked to define God I think a lot of people would use the phrase *pure consciousness*. A lot of religions believe what Deepak believes, that "consciousness is fundamental," that the underlying substratum of all reality is consciousness.

Buddha didn't accept this. For him consciousness was just one of the five elements that come together to form what we call a person. Consciousness is not fundamental. It appears when subject and object interact. It's like an itch. It occurs when two things come together and irritate each other.

But that's not the way most religious people treat it. Instead they tend to adhere to the idea that consciousness is the basis of everything that exists. As far as I understand it, the belief appears to be that everything in the universe is created by consciousness, which is a formless something that just sits there making stuff and experiencing it.

This is the essence of idealistic philosophy. The formless experiential side of reality, the idealists say, is the basis for everything, while the hard materialistic side of reality is negligible. Even though I've already mentioned this before, it bears repeating because it's a very attractive idea. But real experience in the real world is never like that.

A branch of ancient Buddhism is often mislabeled "Buddhist radical idealism," and a lot of people misconstrue it as being an example of the kind of philosophy that Chopra and his followers accept. This branch of Buddhism is usually called Yogacara, which means "the Way of Yoga." Here yoga refers not to stretching exercises but to meditation. The philosophers of the Yogacara school stated that their philosophies were the outcome of their meditation practice.

The Yogacara school died out a few hundred years ago. But much of their philosophy found its way into Zen. Dogen was fond of some of the Yogacara literature, though he was not a Yogacara person himself.

The Yogacara school is sometimes referred to as "mind-only" Buddhism. People who just read those two words and don't delve more deeply into what the Yogacara philosophers said think that those in this school believed that everything in the universe was the product of the mind. That's not the case. Andrew Skilton, in his book *A Concise History of Buddhism*, puts it like this: "What is being said by this school of thought is not that everything is made of mind (as if mind were some kind of universal matter), but that the totality of our experience is dependent upon our mind." This is very different from the belief that consciousness is fundamental or that God is pure consciousness.

This is an important point. On the one hand, any description of reality is fundamentally flawed. So saying that consciousness is the underlying substratum of reality is wrong, and saying it isn't is wrong too. But the belief that ideas are more real than concrete objects is more wrong than saying that both mind and matter are manifestations of something that is neither mind nor matter.

The idea expressed by Deepak that the material world is Maya is an interesting one as well. I remember very clearly sitting in one of Nishijima Roshi's lectures and being shocked when he said, "The material world is an illusion." Up until then I had understood Buddhism to hold the position that the material world was reality. But this is not the case. The material world, in Buddhist terms, is one manifestation of reality. But it isn't the only manifestation of reality. The same goes for consciousness. It's one manifestation of reality, but it isn't reality itself.

Another of the things that Nishijima said in his lectures that really shocked me was, "Consciousness is just an idea." When I heard that, I thought it was pure madness. How could consciousness be just an idea? Up until that moment I had assumed that consciousness was the one thing I could be certain was *not* an idea.

Even the most materialistic of philosophers will, if you press him on the subject, concede that ultimately the only thing we can be certain exists is experience. We may not know quite what we are or what the universe is, but damn it, *something* is experiencing it! You can't deny that. Or if you do deny it based on the duality between that something and what it experiences, at least you have to agree that experience *is*.

For a lot of people, what experiences the universe is a thing they call "consciousness." But then again, some experiences are beyond consciousness. We're unconscious for several hours every night, but we're still alive during that time. And we have dreams that, even though they leave no imprint on our conscious memory, we still experience as if they were really happening. In meditation there are often moments or even long stretches of time in which thoughts, memories, and so forth cease to arise. And yet we experience something then as well. This experience may leave some traces in the memory as having happened. But the content of the experience may as well be nothing since there is no way for conscious memory to retrieve it.

So consciousness is just an idea. We conceive of something we call "consciousness" and assign all kinds of attributes and limitations to it. Like all other ideas we carry around in our heads, consciousness is certain things and is not other things.

I suppose that Chopra would say that since consciousness is fundamental, it is unlimited. If I were to say that my desk is not consciousness, someone who believed that everything was consciousness would have to counter by saying that it actually is.

The idea that consciousness is fundamental or that it is the ultimate form of God can lead us to the wrong conclusions about life. Yet it's a very appealing idea. It leads you to start imagining that consciousness exists eternally, that you will be around to experience everything that happens forever and ever amen.

I must say that I personally like this idea a lot. I love it, in fact! Are you kidding? I'm the biggest sci-fi nerd around. I'd love to believe that I'll somehow experience the time when human beings finally make contact with intelligences beyond planet Earth. And that's only one of the cool things that's bound to happen after Brad Warner types his last book. It would be awesome to be part of all those amazing things.

But I think that belief is both a huge mistake — and yet also kind of true on some level. My experience that day by the Sengawa River as well as other things that have occurred since then have let me know that what I conceive of as Brad Warner is not as small and limited as I'd once believed. In fact, Brad Warner extends beyond the bounds of the universe itself.

But an important caveat must be added to that. Brad Warner does not exist, and never did.

CHAPTER 9

THE MEANING OF LIFE

You're probably wondering what I meant when I stated in the last chapter that "annihilation is the meaning of life." Let me try and explain.

I'm in my car one day driving from Brooklyn, where I was living at the time, down to Knoxville, Tennessee, to visit my sister and her family for Christmas. My dad was coming up from Texas, so it was going to be a big ol' family reunion. And I get a call from my friend Catie down in Durham, North Carolina. And I'm wondering what Catie could possibly want.

It turns out she called me to talk about the meaning of life. It seems that at the end of every year a music and arts paper in Greensboro runs a piece about the meaning of life, and they have various local people contribute their views about the subject. Although I had lived in Chapel Hill for a brief time over the summer, I probably wasn't completely qualified to be called a local. But Catie had talked the editor of the piece into asking me for my take on the subject.

I would be on the road for the next six hours, and they needed my bit before midnight. So Catie arranged for the editor of the paper to call me up and take down my reaction to the question "What is the meaning of life?" as dictation and then turn that into something for the article.

I don't usually like to work this way. I don't even like talking on a cell phone while I drive. It's dangerous. Nobody should do it, ever. Plus, I feel that if you're gonna call yourself a writer you should actually write, not just dictate stuff for other people to turn into something that you then sign off on. But it was important to Catie, so I said okay. Here is what I told the interviewer.

This question about the meaning of life has always been a biggie for me. This is what I got into Zen to try and figure out. My mom dying of Huntington's disease really pushed me into it. I wondered if there could be any meaning to life at all when terrible things happened to completely nice people like my mother. Catie's best friend, Tim LaFollette, inherited Lou Gehrig's disease from his mother. When I was a teenager, before she had died, I learned that I could inherit my mom's condition too. So the question had an urgency for me that I don't think it has for most people. I didn't know if I'd be able to live long enough to figure it out, so I needed to start quick. The reason I stuck with Zen is that, among all the religions and all the philosophies I have encountered, Zen seems to be the one best equipped to answer the question of what life means. It allows you to practice death and thereby find life. The meaning of life is, to me, the meaning of God.

The reason Zen is best equipped to deal with that question is that it doesn't approach it in the same way as other religions or philosophies. Religions generally deal with the question by giving you The Answer. You want to know the meaning of life, kid? Okay. Here it is. It's written down in this book. Memorize this answer, and anytime anyone asks you about the meaning of life, all you have to do is recite it straight out of the book. Problem solved.

I'm well aware that there are religious answers to the question that are quite a bit more nuanced than that. But when I was a teenager the more esoteric branches of religion were not available to me. The religions I encountered all seemed to offer some variation of an easy answer that could be memorized and regurgitated on cue like the answers to the questions on your driving test.

The problem was that when you dug into them even the slightest bit, the answers themselves were always pretty nonsensical. Plus it wasn't good enough to regurgitate the answer from the book. You also needed to have what they called faith. You were supposed to truly believe the answer. But I couldn't comprehend this whole matter of belief, and I still can't. I'm not sure I understand what the word *belief* is even supposed to mean. I'll talk a bit more about belief later. But for now, here's the short version. I believe, for example, that Ohio is a state in the Midwest, that it has cold winters and hot, sticky summers. I believe that men really did land on the moon in 1969 and that there's something more to JFK's assassination than the official version. I don't believe in the tooth fairy, Santa Claus, or transmigration of the soul. So far, so good.

But when it comes to stuff like, for example, believing that Jesus Christ died for my sins, I have a serious problem. The problem is that I don't even know who or what Jesus Christ was or is, what my sins are, or how someone other than me could have died from them. In order for me to believe that Christ died for my sins, I'd have to have a whole other layer of beliefs, perhaps several layers. These involve believing other people's explanations of what, exactly, sins are, who Jesus was, how and why he died for my sins, and on and on. Other belief-based religions present the same problem. To me it seemed a very convoluted way of addressing the meaning of life.

You probably know about the rule they call Occam's razor. It is usually summarized as "the simplest explanation is most likely the correct one." Take the explanation that the Earth orbits the sun. In the Middle Ages the Church tried its best to deny this since it didn't accord with their interpretation of the Bible. But in order to describe what we can observe about the movements of the stars, the changes of the seasons, and so on in terms of the sun orbiting a stationary Earth, we would have to create a lot of really elaborate explanations. If we say that the Earth orbits the sun, the explanations become much simpler.

Therefore, this is the explanation that makes the most sense. It's simple and it's easy to verify.

I didn't want an elaborate explanation of the meaning of life requiring 157 layers of belief in all kinds of things I couldn't possibly verify. And why would God care what I believed, anyhow? Why would that be important to God? That made no sense.

Philosophers offered more nuanced takes on the matter. But those weren't very satisfactory, either. Their answers all seem to involve a lot of intellectual game playing. I'm really not very bright. Often I can't even understand the words used by the philosophers. What the hell is *epistemology*? What is *teleology*? What is *quiddity*?*

It was all very heady stuff. And I was pretty certain that life wasn't lived in the head.

The problem with most variations on the answer to the question "What is the meaning of life?" is that these answers exist outside life itself. You cannot place an intellectual answer on top of something that's too big to be overlaid with such an answer.

The brain is an organ whose job it is to make sense of the world we encounter so that we can operate efficiently. It does this by ignoring most of the input it receives and then slicing the rest into usable chunks. All vertebrates, and many invertebrates, have brains of some sort. And these brains all do the same basic job. Since the human brain is the most complex brain, as far as we know, it does its job in a tremendously detailed way.

Trying to understand the meaning of life in terms of the human brain's activities is like trying to understand the ocean by going to the seashore and scooping out a bucket of water and then analyzing it. You could certainly understand a lot of things about the ocean this way. You could check the saline content of the water, you could see what kinds of microbes lived in it, you might even be lucky enough to scoop up a baby octopus or a fish. But you wouldn't get any information about

---

* Oh, isn't that the game they play in the Harry Potter novels?

the tides, how the ocean affects atmospheric patterns, the fact that the ocean attracts cute girls in bikinis in the summer, and so on.

What you get when you try to understand the meaning of life intellectually is just one tiny slice of life. Even if you understand that tiny slice very thoroughly, you still won't really have understood the fullness of life. Also, any so-called meaning of life you'd grok intellectually would change according to how your life changed. The meaning of life when you're twenty-one wouldn't be the same meaning of life as when you're fifty-one. Maybe on your deathbed you'd end up with something that you might call the ultimate meaning of life, in that it would be the final (ultimate) meaning of life you'd be able to come up with. But even this would be transitional since it would be gone once you died.

In Zen we often say there is no meaning of life. When people first hear that, they think it sounds depressing. It sounds as if we're saying that life is meaningless. But we're not. We're saying that any meaning you assign to life is, by necessity, incomplete. It cannot be otherwise. Trying to assign a meaning to life is like trying to stuff the whole ocean into a bucket.

But you can also say there is a meaning of life. It's another one of those contradictions.

There isn't a meaning of life in terms you could express as "Life means X, Y, and Z." Yet meaning and life are intimately intertwined. Nishijima Roshi often said that there are two aspects of life, matter and meaning. These two aspects, he said, are manifestations of the same thing. It's a different way of saying, "Form is emptiness and emptiness is form."

Matter is matter. It's books and tables and birds and 1962 Fender Jazz Bass guitars and so on. Meaning is that other, more nebulous side of life that can't really be quantified. We experience meaning, so we know it's real, even if we can't weigh or measure it.

But what about when bad things happen to good people? If there really were a meaning of life and if there really was a God, surely my mother and Tim LaFollette would have been spared the suffering they endured. If there really were a God there would be no war, disease, poverty, lousy boy bands, or crappy movies with all-star casts. How can there be any meaning to life if shit like that exists?

I get that. But the God I believe in doesn't perform miracles. (More on that in a later chapter.) And the God I believe in isn't just good, if good is just that which stands in contrast to evil. Joshu Sasaki Roshi, the Japanese Rinzai Zen teacher whom I quoted in the title of this book, said, "You are educated all your life to venerate God and reject evil. Zen education is totally different: it teaches you how to swallow God and the devil at once."

When we talk about bad things happening to good people, using the word *God* can be problematic, as it can be in general. We tend to think of God as an independent agent who can work magic and fix bad situations. We have a long history of thanking God for things we like and cursing the devil for things we hate.

Many modern, rational people generally don't believe in that kind of God. I certainly don't. But we don't need to leap to the conclusion that just because there isn't a giant Santa Claus figure sitting on a throne up in heaven, therefore there is no meaning to life and there is no God.

The life we are leading right now is a manifestation of God. That we are alive is all the evidence we need to prove that God exists. I don't mean that we need to postulate the existence of God to explain the fact that we're here. I'm not talking about God as the first cause of everything. I'm saying that our direct experience of life *is* God. Life is God experiencing God, just as Dogen said when he said we are the eyes and ears "it" uses to experience itself.

As for annihilation, it is one of the crucial aspects of life that makes it what it is. It's a cliché to say that we love our lives more because we know we're going to lose them. But it's not just that we will lose our lives at some undefined time in the future. We lose our lives every second of every day. The nature of the present moment *is* change, *is* annihilation.

It's trendy these days to talk about "the now" and to celebrate the present moment. And that's fine. It's a good trend. But people often forget that the nature of the present moment is the total annihilation of what has gone before. The present moment is highly destructive as well as creative. This is why many of us fear it so much. The present moment is killing us!

But even this is a beautiful thing. The destructive power of the now, of God, is its way of creating us anew at every moment so that we can be here to enjoy its amazingness.

CHAPTER 10

IN WHICH I DISCOVER THE TRUE MEANING OF FAITH BY GOING TO FINLAND

When I think about meaning and faith, I think of Finland.

I was invited there by a guy named Markus, which is pronounced "marrrrkus." You have to roll your *r*'s in Finnish. Markus is a strapping young man, not at all the kind of bespectacled geek-boy one usually associates with people who are into Zen. He's a loud, boisterous, cheerful dude with a wife and three kids. He works as a moving man while attending university at night. He's totally dedicated to Zen practice, sitting zazen every morning and every evening without fail. He even set aside ninety days for a private *ango*, or meditation intensive. Normally an *ango* is something you do with a big group of people, all of whom work together to keep each other on task. Markus did his *ango* alone. I was impressed.

Markus emailed me to say that he wanted me to come to his country. I figured it was yet another one of the many utterly impossible invitations I receive constantly. It's nice that people invite me to come speak in their towns, and I appreciate that they want to hear what I have to say. But it seems like lots of people who invite me imagine I have an entourage of folks who can set everything up and buttloads of money to pay for it all. Unfortunately, I don't.

Markus, though, was willing to formulate a plan, and pretty soon I was on an airplane bound for Helsinki, a place I had never even thought about going to.

It was late summer when I arrived, so I missed Finland's famous snowy winter, as well as its famous endless days when the sun never really sets. I didn't get to encounter that until my next visit a year later, also at Markus's invitation, when I went in June. Still, even in August the sunset was really late and the sunrise was really early, as far as I was concerned.

Markus had arranged a packed schedule for me. The morning after I arrived in Helsinki we set off for the city of Turku, a couple hours' drive to the northwest. A guy named Siike, pronounced "c. k.," was making a documentary of my trip to Finland. He had hoped to find a Finnish distributor but ended up releasing it himself instead. So he tagged along, filming nearly everything I did. Siike never seemed to eat, and he looked like kind of a hippie. So I started joking that he lived on sunshine and good vibes.

Markus showed me the sights of Turku, such as its ancient stone castle, its seaport, its historic downtown. I was pretty impressed. This was a weird and wonderful country. Everyone was tall, blond, and good-looking. In contrast, I felt like a hunched-over little Neanderthal.

While in Finland I found myself thinking a lot about the concept of faith as it exists in Buddhism. Here's why. One of the events that Markus set up for me was a panel discussion in Helsinki with a group of Finland's most distinguished Buddhists. Several of the panelists were from the Helsinki Zen Center, which is part of Philip Kapleau's lineage. One of the others was a famous art critic named J. O. Mallander. But the panelist I most remember was a professor from Helsinki University who was a convert to Tibetan Buddhism.

He was exactly the kind of person I would cast in a movie to play the role of a professor of Buddhism at Helsinki University. He was bald with a full gray beard and little spectacles. He wore a tweed suit with a dark tie. In the diary I kept at the time I described him as looking like a rabbi.

The thing I remember most about him, though, was the way he went on about reincarnation. He said the reason he looked Jewish even though he wasn't was that he had been a Jew in a past life. He apparently knew about several of his former lives, and he referred to them in his talk. He said we ought to be kind to snakes because one of them might have been our grandmother.

I've had to deal with the subject of reincarnation so often that I'm kind of fed up with it. It's one of those things that Westerners who are new to Buddhism seem to find eternally fascinating. I don't. I find it exhausting. But I have to talk about it all the time anyway.

We all want to believe in life after death. Even most of the people who don't believe in life after death will say they would *like* to believe in it, when you really press them. Hell, even I would *like* to believe in it! But according to Dogen, reincarnation is a non-Buddhist idea introduced into Buddhism after Buddha was dead and gone and couldn't complain about it. In the *Shobogenzo* chapter titled "A Talk about Pursuing the Truth" ("*Bendowa*" in Japanese), he says, "According to the non-Buddhist view, there is one spiritual intelligence existing within our body. When this body dies, however, the spirit casts off the skin and is reborn on the other side; so even though it seems to die here it lives on there. Therefore we call it immortal and eternal. But if we learn this view as the Buddha's Dharma, we are even more foolish than the person who grasps a tile or a pebble thinking it to be a golden treasure."

That being said, there are other parts of *Shobogenzo* in which Dogen appears to believe in something like rebirth. He talks about ancient masters who knew hundreds of past lives,* he talks about how your karma can follow you into future lifetimes,† he even says that after you die you should continuously chant a certain Buddhist mantra during

---

* In the *Shobogenzo* chapter "Deep Belief in Cause and Effect," or "*Shin Jin Inga*" in Japanese.
† In "Karma in the Three Times," or "*San Ji No Go*" in Japanese.

"Middle Existence," which is the time between your death in one life-time and your rebirth in the next.*

But in all these instances he appears to be using the ideas about rebirth that were common among his listeners to make other points. The thing about knowing hundreds of past lives is used to illustrate how useless so-called supernatural powers are. The thing about karma following you into future lives is used to illustrate how vital it is to behave morally in the present. The thing about chanting that mantra during Middle Existence is used to illustrate how important it is to respect the Buddhist teachings since the mantra he talks about is one of reverence to them. Whenever Dogen writes directly about rebirth or reincarnation rather than referring to it obliquely when talking about something else, he is very clearly not a fan.

The concepts of life after death and God seem to be inextricably bound together. If there is a God, many say, then there is life after death. If there is no God, then there can't be life after death. That appears to be the usual reasoning.

Life after death is a matter of faith. I know there are people out there who claim it's a matter of experience because they've heard of that kid who died and supposedly went to heaven and then wrote a book about it, which you can buy at any supermarket or gas station. Some, like that Finnish professor, claim to remember their previous incarnations. In the traditional version of Buddha's life story, his enlightenment is preceded by a moment in which he is able to remember all of his former lives and see how insubstantial they were.

But there is no way to know whether these stories — even the ones about Buddha — are true. Some say the stuff about Buddha's past lives was a later interpolation by people who wanted Buddhism to be more palatable to Hindus, who have a strong belief in reincarnation. Others insist it was Buddha's actual testimony. In any case, I don't see how it matters much either way. Some say you need the concept of past and

---

* In "The Will to the Truth," or "*Doshin*" in Japanese.

future lives in order to make the idea of karma work out. If everything we do has karmic consequences, then why do bad things happen to good people and good things happen to bad people? If those good people were bad in past lives and vice versa, it all works out. But this appears to me to be just wishful speculation and, as such, not very useful. I don't really see the need to believe in reincarnation in order to make the idea of karma plausible. When I've quietly observed my own real life I see it working all the time. I will come back to this idea a bit later.

As for contemporary stories of people who recall their previous lives, I find most of them unconvincing. I mean, how many Napoleons and Christs and Cleopatras and Joan of Arcs were there? Hardly anyone who recalls a previous life ever remembers anything mundane. And that kid who went to heaven? I'm sure his evangelist father had no hand in guiding his son's recollections. Uh-huh. Most of the purported instances of people having verifiable evidence of past lives fall apart on closer examination. So we're left with only faith to guide us.

When I was younger, I really wanted to understand just what this word *faith* meant. The Christians I encountered as a kid in rural Ohio tried to explain it to me. They said that if you believed that Jesus really rose from the dead, that Noah really did put two of every animal onto a real boat, that Moses really did part the Red Sea, then you had faith. So the best I could make of their explanations was that faith was a belief in things that didn't make much sense and for which there was no real evidence.

In her book *A Case for God* Karen Armstrong explains that the words *faith* and *belief* didn't always mean what they mean when used by mainstream Christians today. "The word translated as 'faith' in the New Testament," she says, "is the Greek *psistis*, which means 'trust; loyalty; engagement; commitment.' Jesus was not asking people to believe in his divinity because he made no such claim. He was asking for commitment."

The word *belief*, as contemporary English speakers use it, is a more recent invention. Originally it meant something more like the Greek word *psistis*. Then it began to change. "In the seventeenth century," Armstrong says, "as our concept of knowledge became more theoretical, the word 'belief' started to be used to describe an intellectual assent to a hypothetical — and often dubious — proposition." Scientists and philosophers started to adopt it, thereby shaping the word's meaning into its current form.

There's also a more esoteric sort of faith, which is harder to pin down. You don't have to believe the Bible is literally true, in the modern sense of that phrase — meaning that if you could go back in a time machine and videotape the event, then it was literally true. There are Christians today who reject that and believe that the Bible may be largely metaphorical and allegorical. But most in that group whom I've encountered seem to feel that you still have to believe that God is real, even though you can't see him and even though a lot of what goes down in the world seems to fly in the face of the idea of a loving God who protects and cares for his creations.

The acclaimed Buddhist author Stephen Batchelor has some strong opinions on this kind of faith as it applies to Buddhism. He rejects both the idea of God and the Buddhist notion of karma as well as its cousin, reincarnation, as what he calls "consolatory belief," or belief in things that just make you feel good, even though there's no real evidence for them. In a video interview posted on YouTube he says, "The problem with the God theory and the karma theory is that it explains everything. In a sense it explains nothing. I personally cannot accept that sort of metaphysical belief in things I can neither prove nor disprove."

Batchelor sees Buddhism as a rational philosophy that teaches us "how to open our hearts and minds to the world as it is and to respond to that authentically." I agree with him, but I do think that Buddhism, even Zen Buddhism, contains an element of faith.

This statement makes some people extremely uncomfortable. It's another one of those cases where people who have come to Buddhism as a way to escape from whatever religion they have rejected often feel like they've been victims of a clever bait and switch.

My first Buddhist teacher, Tim McCarthy, used to say that to be a Buddhist you had to have an equal amount of doubt and faith. This, to me, is the key. If all you have is doubt you're likely to get cynical and give up. If all you have is faith you're likely to go off the deep end and believe all kinds of crazy stuff just because it's somehow appealing.

When you first encounter Buddhism, there are all these concepts you can't really understand. I'm not talking about things like reincarnation. There are subtler matters than that. For example, what do you do when you first encounter lines like "Form is emptiness, emptiness is form" in the Heart Sutra?

At first it just doesn't make much sense. But if you sit and think about it for a minute it seems to go against everything you've been taught since childhood. Form is quite clearly different from emptiness. What makes form form is the fact that it is not emptiness. That's the definition of form and the definition of emptiness. They are in complete contradistinction to each other. It's like saying that a brand-new Porsche is the same thing as a weed-strewn driveway with no car in it. It's demonstrably untrue.

Yet part of Buddhist practice is that we accept things like this on faith. We have faith that if we continue the practice long enough and sincerely enough, these kinds of things will start to make sense. It's not that we'll become so indoctrinated with the belief system that we cease to question it. Zen practice has no element of indoctrination, and what you choose to believe is not considered significant in any way. The practice of stripping away belief, they say, will make the underlying truth about reality clear. I know this for myself now. But at first I had to take it on faith.

In my own case, the kind of faith I'm talking about is synonymous with trust, much in the way the early followers of Jesus used the word *faith* (*psistis*). I trusted that my teachers were neither delusional nor lying to me. This was easy enough to do because they were people I knew personally and could interact with. But I also trusted people I didn't know. I trusted the words of Shunryu Suzuki, who died when I was just a little kid, and the words of Dogen, who died seven hundred years before I was born. I couldn't verify that they weren't liars or delusional people based on personal observation of their behavior the way I could with my teachers. But something in the way they wrote convinced me that they were worthy of my faith.

It's impossible for me to say why I had such faith. Rationally speaking, I was certain that neither Tim McCarthy nor Nishijima Roshi was attempting to brainwash me into joining some weird cult. That's a real danger because a good cult leader can skillfully manipulate a vulnerable person's desire to trust. But if either Tim or Nishijima was leading a cult, they were the most ineffectual, disorganized cults ever. Epic fail.

Human beings are social animals. Even hermits and wandering ascetics need some kind of minimal interaction with others of their species to survive. No matter how much I pride myself on my individualism, I know that I need other people. I didn't make the computer I'm typing this on. I didn't build the apartment I'm living in. I don't run the subway system. I don't grow my own food. I am not really independent at all.

Faith is built into the human social system. If I go to a doctor and she gives me some pills, I need to have a certain amount of faith that she's not giving me poison, that her diagnosis is sound, and that the medicine has some chance of being effective. Studies show that this kind of faith plays an important role in healing.

This is the kind of faith required in Buddhism, faith mixed with doubt. I have faith in my doctor. But I also know she could be wrong. She could be lazy in her diagnosis. She could be unaware that there's a better medication than the ones she routinely prescribes. The list goes on. But at some point I have to put my trust in her. Or, if not in her, then in someone else whom I have more reason to trust.

This is not blind faith that would have us believe in things because they are spoken by someone with authority. Buddha himself cautioned against that in a famous speech known to us today as the Kalama Sutra. He said we should not go by what has been written in scripture or spoken by an authority figure. We need to see for ourselves what is true and what works. We need to learn from our own experience.

But when it comes to meditation, it's often hard for people to have that kind of faith. How do you know when you're first getting into it that a meditation practice is going to be worth the considerable investment of time and effort? It is not at all clear from the start. For all you know, you might meditate every day for years and years, only to realize at some point that the whole thing has been a complete waste of time.

A lot of people worry about that at the outset of their practice. In response to this a few meditation teachers these days are advocating techniques that supposedly give a person a taste of the enlightened state very quickly. The idea is that these people will then be encouraged to pursue the practice seriously until they have deeper experiences later on.

As attractive as this idea may sound, it's utter nonsense. It's based on the notion that enlightenment is some kind of extraordinary state, like the states you can achieve by taking hallucinogenic drugs. But as I said before, enlightenment is actually your normal, natural state. It's the state you are in at this very moment. If there is any aim to zazen practice, the aim is to teach you how to be quiet enough to stop chasing after extraordinary states and simply notice who and what you are right now.

I knew that zazen would not be a waste of my time because I met teachers who had practiced it and in whom I could see the effects of practice. It is not that either of my teachers were what one would call perfect beings. But they were perfectly themselves. And that was important, because it's so very rare.

In the *Shobogenzo* chapter "Flowers in Space" ("*Kuge*" in Japanese), Dogen quotes Buddha as saying, "It is like a person who has clouded eyes seeing flowers in space. If the sickness of clouded eyes is cured, flowers vanish in space." In his comments on this Dogen says, "Do not stupidly see cloudedness as delusion and learn that true reality exists elsewhere. To do so would be the small view. If cloudedness and flowers were delusion, that which attaches to the wrong view that they are delusion, and the attachment itself, must all be delusion."

The common approach to meditation is to envision the state we wish to achieve with our meditation and make efforts to attain that state. We know that we have clouded eyes, and we imagine what the world might look like without all those clouds in the way. But our image of enlightenment is based on our delusion.

Dogen's approach was completely different. He was interested in seeing deeply into his real state as it was right here and right now — clouds and all. You don't need some kind of "quick taste of enlightenment" to do this. In fact, anything along those lines will only deepen your delusion by making you think that the imaginary version of enlightenment you've created out of your own delusions is real.

In the end I can't create faith in you by guaranteeing that meditation practice will produce the results you desire. Quite the opposite. In my experience zazen has not produced anything like the results I desired when I first started the practice. Dogen said, "When you realize buddhadharma,* you do not think, 'This is realization just as I expected.' Even if you think so, realization invariably differs from your expectation. Realization is not like your conception of it."†

Since I say that I have faith in Buddha and faith in God, you might wonder whether Buddha *is* God. Let's look at that question next, shall we?

---

* "The way of the Buddha."
† From the *Shobogenzo* chapter "Buddhas Alone Together with Buddhas," or "*Yuibutsu Yobutsu*" in Japanese.

CHAPTER 11

IS BUDDHA GOD?

In the Lotus Sutra, Shakyamuni Buddha says,

> Now this triple world
> All is my possession
> And living beings in it
> All are my children.

Sounds as though he's claiming to be God, doesn't it? Jesus made the same sort of claim in John 10:30 when he said, "I and my Father are one," and in John 17:5 when he said, "And now, O Father, glorify thou me with thine own self with the glory which I had with thee before the world was." And look what happened with him! Lots of people took him at his word and said, "That guy Jesus over there is God. I'm not God, but he is. So I'm going to worship him. And furthermore, I'm going to give anybody who doesn't agree a very hard time."

Both the Gospel of John and the Lotus Sutra, though they claim to record the words of Jesus and Shakyamuni (the historical Buddha), respectively, are historically suspect. Passages from the Lotus Sutra first began to appear around 400 years after Shakyamuni died, and the full sutra itself doesn't seem to have existed until around 200 CE, some 700 years after Shakyamuni was dead, gone, and had his teeth and bones scattered into stupas all over Asia. The Gospel of John was the last of the gospels to be written and appears to date anywhere from 90 to 120 years after Jesus left this world, perhaps even considerably later. Interestingly enough, both these works appear to have been composed around the same general time period, though the Gospel of John is historically much closer to the time of Jesus than the Lotus Sutra is to the time of Shakyamuni.

One of the cornerstones of contemporary mainstream Christian faith is that Jesus is God. The rest of us are not God, but Jesus is. Jesus is, therefore, a very special person, to say the least. This probably wasn't always the way Jesus's followers thought of him. But it's pretty much the norm today. Buddhism, in spite of passages like the one quoted above and others like it, has never held the idea that Shakyamuni Buddha was God, at least not in the sense that he alone was God and the rest of us schmucks are not.

Having said this, I am well aware that you can find branches of Buddhism in which people do believe that Shakyamuni Buddha was some kind of supernatural being. You could make a strong case that there are Buddhists who regard Shakyamuni as *a* god or even as *the* God of their religion. To give you just one example, I have encountered some Thai Buddhists who seemed to regard Shakyamuni Buddha as God in much the same way that Christians regard Jesus Christ as God.

For more than a decade I worked at Tsuburaya Productions in Tokyo, Japan. Tsuburaya made monster movies and TV shows. They were particularly famous for a TV series called *Ultraman*. Ultraman is a jumbo-sized superhero, forty meters (131.23 feet) tall. He battles gigantic Godzilla-type monsters. The show is not an animated cartoon. The superhero vs. monster battles are portrayed by men wearing weird costumes duking it out on miniaturized models of Tokyo.

During my work at Tsuburaya I met a group of movie business-people from Thailand, the leader of whom said he was a Buddhist monk. During my conversations with this Thai gentleman and his son, it came up that I too was a Buddhist monk. After speaking with them it became quite clear that their ideas of Buddhism were enormously different from mine.

I did some research and discovered that a lot of (what I would consider) strange things are associated with Buddhism in Thailand. There are stories of wonder-working saints, there are faith healers, and there's the belief that Buddha can be petitioned to bend the laws of cause and effect to perform miracles on behalf of the faithful. The Thai gentleman in question had even made movies in which gigantic Buddhist deities portrayed by men in bad costumes smooshed evil-doers underfoot as they ran for cover. So when Western Buddhist teachers claim, as they often do, that Buddhists never worship Buddha as a God, they're leaving some things out.

A guy named David L. McMahan has written a very good book called *The Making of Buddhist Modernism.* In it he says that the way Buddhism is usually presented in the West today may not give us a true portrait of the way Buddhism was understood in other times or even of how it is understood in contemporary Asia. This isn't just because Western teachers like me have misunderstood Buddhism on account of our cultural conditioning. In fact, he says, many prominent Asian teachers have been just as influenced by modern Westernized thinking.

McMahan believes that this is a natural progression and completely consistent with the original intent of Buddha himself. I agree. I feel that Buddhism is sort of like advanced physics. Albert Einstein pioneered so much of advanced physics it might be somehow appropriate to call it "Einsteinism" as a way of honoring his contributions to the field. But even if we did change the name of advanced physics to Einsteinism we would not be saying that anything that came after Einstein's death is not legitimate. Similarly, we use the word *Buddhism* as a way to honor the founder of the philosophy. But we would no more want to freeze Buddhism by adhering only to what the historical Buddha said than physicists would want to freeze physics by adhering only to what Einstein said.

People worry far too much about the Westernization and modernization of Buddhism. For example, it's nice to have faithful versions of ancient Buddhist texts. But we also have to be aware that even the most faithful versions we produce are not faithful. Even if we read the texts in their original languages, we come from such a different place culturally that we still won't be able to understand what the people who wrote them meant exactly. The people who read those texts during the authors' lifetimes may not have fully understood what their writers meant. Our own language, English, didn't even exist at the time most of those texts were written.

McMahan, in fact, cites a passage by Jay Garfield regarding the subject of translation:

> When we translate, we transform in all of the following ways: we replace terms and phrases with particular sets of resonances in their source language with terms and phrases with very different resonances in the target language; we disambiguate ambiguous terms, and introduce new ambiguities; we interpret, or fix particular interpretations of texts in virtue of the use of theoretically loaded expressions in our target language; we take a text that is to some extent esoteric and render it exoteric simply by freeing the target language reader to approach the text without a teacher; we shift the context in which a text is read and used.

McMahan talks about the way the Sanskrit word *moksha* is translated as "freedom." While this is not an entirely inappropriate translation, *moksha* means, in McMahan's words, "liberation from rebirth in samsara as an embodied being, as well as liberation from destructive mental states (*klesas*), craving, hatred, and delusion and from the suffering (*dukha*) they produce."

On the other hand, he says, the English word *freedom* conveys to Western readers such things as "individual freedom, creative freedom, freedom of choice, freedom from oppression, freedom of thought, freedom of speech, freedom from neuroses, free to be me — let freedom ring" and so on. So while "freedom" is a proper translation of *moksha*, it still means something very different.

So the question of whether or not Buddhism outside contemporary Western culture regards Buddha as being supernatural can come with a very complicated answer. But we can say for certain that Buddha never claimed to be God or a prophet of God and furthermore that he did not regard the question of the existence or nonexistence of God as very important.

In the *Majjhima Nikaya*, the "Collection of Middle Length Discourses," he famously said, "Suppose someone was hit by a poisoned arrow and his friends and relatives found a doctor able to remove the arrow. If this man were to say, 'I will not have this arrow taken out until I know whether the person who had shot it was a priest, a prince or a merchant, his name and his family. I will not have it taken out until I know what kind of bow was used and whether the arrowhead was an ordinary one or an iron one.' That person would die before all these things are ever known to him."

He considered things like knowing the origin of the world and who created it to be equally unimportant. The answers didn't matter. It was our suffering here and now that mattered. Buddha believed that we need to deal with the practical questions of how to live in this world now. Worrying about who created it and suchlike is the same as worrying about gay marriage when we have a financial meltdown and a health care crisis to deal with. It's a case of wasting time and energy on something that doesn't matter while ignoring the things that really do.

Still, in the passage I quoted from the Lotus Sutra above we have a statement that, in spite of its dubious historical origins, is regarded by many if not most Buddhists as being an accurate expression of what Shakyamuni actually taught. It is regarded as authentically Buddhist by most adherents of the Zen sect, even though most of us believe the Lotus Sutra is of historically dubious origins.

Dogen talks about this passage in a chapter from *Shobogenzo* titled

"The Triple World Is Mind Alone" ("*Sangai-Yuishin*" in Japanese). The phrase *triple world* comes up a lot in Buddhist teaching, and it has a few related meanings. Sometimes it means "the world of thinking, feeling, and action." Other times it means "the world of volition, matter, and nonmatter." Still other times it means "past, present, and future."

In every case, though, it indicates the world we are living in here and now. In the world here and now, thinking, feeling, and action all take place. It is the only place where these things can actually happen. This world is also a world of matter, nonmatter, and volition. Matter and volition are obvious. Nonmatter refers to those aspects of the world that are nonmaterial but still obvious and real, such as our thoughts, our feelings, our sensations, our attitudes, and so forth. As for the past, present, and future, these are also bound up in this moment. We are the product of our past actions, we are present right now, and we have a future that depends on what we do in this moment.

In his introduction to this chapter in his translation of *Shobogenzo*, Nishijima Roshi summarizes Dogen's attitude like this: "The phrase refers to the teaching that reality exists in the contact between subject and object. From this viewpoint, when we say that the world is only the mind, we also need to say that the mind is only the world, to express the fact that the relationship is a mutual one."*

"The triple world has no outside," Dogen says. He quotes Shakyamuni from the Lotus Sutra as saying, "The doctrine that there is another world of living beings outside the triple world is a non-Buddhist doctrine." This is an important concept if you want to understand the Buddhist attitude toward God.

In most religions that I'm aware of, God operates in the universe from a position somewhere removed from it. He can stick his hand into the universe like a kid sticking his hand into the cage he keeps his iguanas in and make things like floods and partings of the sea and resurrections happen. Apparently many Americans these days believe God can

---

* Take *that*, Deepak Chopra!

even make certain football teams beat certain other football teams. But he does this from a position outside the things he interacts with.

This is not the stance taken by Buddhist philosophy. Buddhism proceeds from the standpoint that the claim of there being anything or anyone outside the universe is absurd. Dogen goes even further than this, though. He says, "The Tathagata [Buddha] has no outside in the same way as fences and walls have no outside. Just as the triple world has no outside, living beings have no outside."

If this doesn't sound absurd to you, it ought to. Fences and walls have an outside. You paint the outside of a wall. You put the electrical wiring inside. There is a clear distinction. Living beings obviously have an outside. If we didn't we'd be in big trouble when we went in for a hernia operation!

But here Dogen is indicating an aspect of our everyday experience that we don't usually notice. He says, "The mind alone is beyond one or two; it is beyond the triple world and beyond leaving the triple world; it is free of error; it has thinking, sensing, mindfulness and realization; it is fences, walls, tiles and pebbles and it is mountains, rivers and the Earth. The mind itself is skin, flesh, bones and marrow."

You can see that the Buddhist idea of mind doesn't just refer to abstract things that occur inside the brain. As Nishijima would say, "Mind is matter and matter is mind."

This idea of leaving the triple world needs some explaining. The phrase appears several times in the Lotus Sutra. It is one way of expressing our relationship to the world. It doesn't mean that we literally escape the real world and go somewhere else. Dogen says "leaving the triple world" and understanding that the triple world is here and now are the same thing. In other words, when we get free of the concept of the triple world by leaving it behind we have a real experience of the triple world being here and now. The concept expresses something about our real life here and now, but even though it's true, it's still just an idea.

In mainstream Christian terms, Jesus, being a special manifestation of God, is seen as being the one and only center of the universe. But consider that we know a lot more about the universe now than anyone knew in the days when Christianity began taking shape. Back in those days the idea that there could be a single center of the Earth made sense. The Earth was seen as a flat surface with specific dimensions. The Earth, it was believed, had ends, though nobody was quite certain where they were. Thus, there would have to be a single spot that was literally the center of the Earth. For early Christians, it was assumed to be Jerusalem.

From my experiences there I can say that Jerusalem is the center of a lot of things, like political intrigue, religious bickering, and hundreds of interesting tourist traps with lots of cheap plastic Christian icons imported from sweatshops in China. But it's not the center of the Earth, except in some deluded people's minds.

Nowadays we understand more about the shape of the Earth and we understand that the idea of there being a center to it makes no real sense, except maybe way down deep underground, but that's not what people meant back in biblical times. In the same sense that there is no center of the Earth, there is no center of the universe. Some say the universe is infinite. Others say it curves back in on itself in four-dimensional space. But in either case there ain't no center.

In Buddhist terms, each and every one of us is the center of the universe. Dogen says, "Because the triple world is the whole universe, 'here and now' is the past, present, and future. The reality of past, present, and future does not obstruct 'the here and now.' The reality of 'the here and now' blocks off past, present, and future."

Here and now in this sense includes our own existence as individuals. We are not simply beings who live in the here and now; we are expressions of here and now. Here and now is not separate from us. We do not obstruct the reality of the entire universe. But in a different sense we block it off.

Notice that in Dogen's quote above, even the present is said to be "blocked off." Robyn Hitchcock, the singer I mentioned earlier, once described infinity in terms of holding up a mirror while standing in front of another mirror. It feels like you could see to infinity, he said, if only your own head didn't keep blocking it off. Dogen is referring to something like the same idea.

It is precisely because we are the center of the universe that we feel isolated within it. We are unable to see the way in which we extend to the ends of the universe. Sometimes we can have a deep intuitive sense of this, though. It is this kind of deep intuitive sense of our profound interconnectedness with the universe that is sometimes mistakenly called Buddha's "enlightenment experience" and is thought to either be unique to Buddha or something that only certain very special people can attain. If it were like that, maybe Buddha would be a god. But it's not.

Dogen again quotes Shakyamuni Buddha from the Lotus Sutra as saying, "The whole universe in ten directions is a real human body." In other words, our own bodies are the entire universe. This is another one of those really strange-sounding ideas you come across in Buddhism. Initially it makes no sense at all. It sounds poetic or metaphorical. Or else it sounds like a reference to something lying outside our own experience or even outside our own ability to experience it.

I looked at it this way myself for a very long time. After a while I just put aside ideas like this as being completely out of my reach. I continued to practice zazen every day because I could see that it did me some practical good. It made me more at ease with myself, it felt nice, it certainly didn't do any harm. But it didn't provide me with any of the kinds of mystical revelations you always read about.

And then one day it did. But my experience wasn't mystical or elevated. It was a moment of deep understanding of exactly what it was to live my normal, day-to-day life just as it was, just as it is. Dogen says, "Without being given, this state is received and without being taken by force this state is acquired." It is our God-given natural state. And yet because we are not accustomed to it, it appears to be extraordinary.

At the moment it happened there by the Sengawa River on that random day, two phrases I had heard from my teachers and had consigned to the area of "things I will never understand" suddenly made perfect sense. Nishijima once told me, "My personality extends throughout the universe." And Tim McCarthy once said, "It [the universe] is more you than you could ever be."

I had remembered those phrases mostly because they were so deeply absurd. Nishijima's statement sounded ridiculously grandiose. And Tim's statement just sounded plain ridiculous. It made no sense to me at all. And yet it stuck in my head, perhaps for that reason alone. Shakyamuni's statement "Now this triple world, all is my possession. And living beings in it, all are my children" can be taken in much the same way as these statements. Whether Shakyamuni himself actually said it or not, someone did. And he was trying to capture in words the profound experience of simply being alive as you are right in this very moment.

CHAPTER 12

SAM HARRIS BELIEVES IN GOD

So Buddha's not God. Or maybe to some people he is. A lot of people have a lot of different ways of defining God. It turns out that even some atheists believe in God. In January 2011 several people forwarded me the same TED Talk about this by Sam Harris. Sam Harris is the best-selling author of the books *The End of Faith* and *The Moral Landscape*. Both these books are considered part of the burgeoning neoatheist movement, and Harris is one of the darlings of that particular scene. In 2005 Harris wrote an article for the *Huffington Post* titled "There Is No God (And You Know It)."

But Harris has a shocking secret. Or so some would have us believe. The television show *Nightline* revealed in the kind of hushed tones usually reserved for divulging some celebrity's scandalous sex secrets that Harris believes that spiritual experience is real. And, they said, Harris (gasp!) *meditates*. At the end of the piece reporter Bill Weir, who filed the story, promised that Harris was about to unveil his greatest innovation. "In it, he plans to lay out a new sort of spirituality [emphatic pause], one devoid of God."

According to *Newsweek*, in a piece titled "Sam Harris Believes in God," "Sam Harris — a hero to the growing numbers of Americans who check the atheist box on opinion polls — concedes he believes in something certain people would call 'God.' In a related thought, he raises the topic of his next project: a spirituality guide tentatively titled *The Illusion of the Self*. Based on Harris's own 'spiritual journey,' it will '[celebrate] the spiritual aspect of human existence [and explain] how we can live moral and spiritual lives without religion,' according to a statement from his publisher, Free Press."

I like Sam Harris's books. But whenever something like this comes out it annoys me no end. It reminds me of when the band Nirvana first came on the scene. Nirvana was a tremendous rock band, and Kurt Cobain was a brilliant songwriter, able to concoct simple catchy tunes that expressed something really deep. What I hated about Nirvana had nothing to do with the band itself. It was the way so many people seemed to believe that Nirvana had spontaneously invented something entirely unprecedented. They didn't catch the fact that the band's sound was largely copped from the Pixies, that their stage antics dated back to The Who's act in the midsixties, that they mined the hardcore punk scene of the early 1980s for much of their clothing style, and so on.

I suppose you could call a spirituality that is devoid of God and that emphasizes that self is an illusion "new" if you're talking in terms of geologic time, since in those terms 2,500 years is just a drop in the bucket. But Buddhists have been working on a spirituality devoid of God — at least in the sense that God appears to be defined by the people reporting this story — ever since Gautama Buddha first laid out the philosophy five hundred years before Christ.

I can understand why Harris might want to distance himself from the "growing numbers of Americans who check the atheist box on opinion polls." I do too. Much of the contemporary American atheist movement seems to be treating atheism as a new kind of religion. Bill Maher said, "Atheism is a religion the same way abstinence is a sex position." It's just that some atheists are so damned evangelical about their nonreligion they might as well be ringing doorbells and handing out leaflets.

Harris would appear to concur, at least in part. In an interview on *Nightline* in December 2010, he said, "If we by definition ignore [spiritual experiences] because of their entanglement with religion we appear less wise than even the craziest of our religious opponents."

Religious language provides us with a way of communicating our spiritual experiences. And just as in any other sphere of human interaction the word is not the thing. A rhinoceros is not a rhinoceros, as a Zen koan might have it — if there were any Zen koans about rhinoceroses. The word *rhinoceros* cannot charge at your car in the safari park and leave a big hole in the fender.

When a person has a deeply spiritual experience and tries to communicate that experience to others, she will use the language her culture has available to express it. Often the only words to be had are those created by the prevailing religion of the culture. When someone else who has had a similar experience hears these words, he might be able to relate to them at more or less the same level. But when someone who has not had such an experience hears these words he's likely to completely misconstrue them. Or, worse yet, he's likely to take them literally.

In many cultures, perhaps even most, spirituality is indeed entangled with religion, as Harris says. The two are so thoroughly intertwined that it often seems impossible to separate one from the other. Some folks these days like to define themselves as spiritual but not religious. But I don't even like the word *spirituality*, since it tends to refer to the way most religions define the spiritual side of our experience as higher or worthier than the material side.

Our languages all proceed from mistaken assumptions. When one speaks about spiritual experiences in English one has to say that *I* had an experience and that it *happened* to *me*. This is because the English language makes certain assumptions about the nature of reality. These assumptions include the idea that there is a "me" to which things "happen" and that these things, after they've occurred, can be called "experiences." English is not the only language that makes these assumptions. All human languages do to some extent. But in some languages it is more evident than in others.

Our linguistic assumptions are often thought to represent the actual limits of reality. When I attempt to express some of the experiences I've had (note the language I'm forced to use), I will sometimes say that the experiences happened and are happening throughout time and space to everyone and everything in the universe. This is linguistically absurd. And because it can't fit our linguistic conceits, some would say such a thing is impossible.

Dogen talks about how we take the poetic language used to express such experiences and twist it into something it's not. In *Shobogenzo* he quotes a very old Zen story about Nagarjuna, a great Buddhist monk and author, "manifesting the form of the moon" while in meditation. The story goes like this:

> The fourteenth patriarch, the Venerable Nagarjuna, is a man from western India, and he goes to southern India. Most people of that nation believe in karma for happiness. The Venerable One [Nagarjuna] preaches for them the subtle Dharma. Those who hear him say to each other, "The most important thing in the human world is that people possess karma for happiness. Yet he talks idly of the buddha-nature. Who can see such a thing?"
>
> The Venerable One says, "If you want to realize the buddha-nature, you must first get rid of selfish pride." The people say, "Is the buddha-nature big or is it small?"
>
> The Venerable One says, "The buddha-nature is not big and not small, it is not wide and not narrow, it is without happiness and without rewards, it does not die and it is not born."
>
> When they hear these excellent principles, they all turn from their original mind. Then the Venerable One, from his seat, manifests his free body, which seems like the perfect circle of a full moon. All those gathered only hear the sound of Dharma; they do not see the master's form. In that assembly is a rich man's son, Kanadeva. He says to the assembly, "Do you know what this form is or not?"
>
> Those in the assembly say, "The present [form] is something

our eyes have never before seen, our ears have never before heard, our minds have never before known, and our bodies have never before experienced."

Kaṇadeva says, "Here the Venerable One is manifesting the form of the buddha-nature to show it to us. How do we know this? It may be presumed that the formless state of samadhi in shape resembles the full moon. The meaning of the buddha-nature is evident and it is transparently clear."

After these words, the circle disappears at once, and [the master] is sitting on his seat. Then he preaches the following verse:

[My] body manifests the roundness of the moon,
By this means demonstrating the physique of the buddhas.
The preaching of Dharma has no set form.
The real function is beyond sounds and sights.

Dogen tells a story about being in China and coming across a painting depicting this scene. The artist had drawn Nagarjuna transforming himself into a big sphere. Dogen criticizes this painting at length as taking Nagarjuna's metaphorical explanation far too literally. He says the artist should have just drawn Nagarjuna as a fully human monk sitting on his cushion. So this confusion about taking things too literally isn't just an invention by Protestants of twentieth- and twenty-first-century America. It transcends cultures and has endured for a very long time.

Now that Sam Harris, the acclaimed champion of the atheist cause, is talking about spirituality and belief in God, some of the atheists in his audience are deeply troubled. Like the religious people they oppose, they have a terrible fear of the unknown and of the unknowable. We all do. I sure do! It's a survival skill we learn very early on. We need to know as much about our environment as possible because what we do not know is potentially dangerous. I don't regard people who fear the unknown and the unknowable as weak or stupid. I regard them as companions, as people who fear pretty much the same things I fear.

Some religious people try to deal with their fear of the unknown and the unknowable by believing in what others have said and written about the unknowable in ancient books. Many in the atheist camp want to deal with their fear of the unknown and the unknowable by believing in what others have said about them in more recent books. If they believe that all spiritual experience is based on hallucinations or imbalanced brain chemistry, then they have nailed it and it is no longer unknown and, therefore, no longer scary.

But do we really understand a thing just because we have given it a name and an explanation? This question can be applied not just to the Great Unknown but to things we encounter all the time. Some people like to use the word *mundane* to describe the things they know. Spiritual people are often seeking that which is beyond the mundane. The mundane is bad, painful, and, worse still, boring. But whatever lies beyond, well, that's where the real action is!

The word *mundane* has all kinds of negative connotations: dull, routine, commonplace, humdrum, and dreary. If that's how you view the world you're living in, you may not actually understand it very well. But I sympathize with you completely. Because that's how I viewed the world for a very long time.

It didn't help that I grew up mainly in Wadsworth, Ohio, the most mundane place in this mundane world. It's a suburb of Akron, Ohio, so even the nearest "big city" was pretty dull.

But I'm sitting in an apartment in Akron right now writing this chapter, and you know what? This is not a mundane place at all. There may not be much going on the way stuff goes on in bigger cities. But this is reality. It's concrete. It's here. Any other place I might think of is unreal. And that's what makes the mundane world not so mundane after all.

As I've touched on already, one difficulty with believing in God may be the word *God* itself. In an interview published by *Newsweek* on October 10, 2010, Harris says, "There's a real problem with the word because it shields the genuinely divisive doctrines and believers from criticism." He says that the way the word *God* is used by about 25 percent of people is reasonable. He doesn't say how he arrived at this figure. But I guess that he is referring to the portion of folks who mean God as a transcendent aspect of the universe. "If the God of the 25 percent is incredibly valuable, which it is; and it's actually worth realizing, which it is; and it's something we can talk about rationally, which it is; then calling it 'God' prevents you from criticizing all the divisive nonsense that comes with religion."

I agree with Harris. And yet I feel that *God* is at best a lousy word to refer to whatever *it* is. It's sort of like the guy who described Nagarjuna's posture as manifesting the roundness of the moon. He was making the best of a bad situation, attempting to force into words something that cannot be described that way.

But that doesn't mean people won't still try and define God. It's in our nature to define things. A lot of people define God as the ultimate arbitrator of moral behavior, and a belief in God, they say, is the only way to keep people from doing bad things. I'd like to talk about this next.

CHAPTER 13

MORALITY AND KARMA

Because I can't seem to get enough of the guy, I want to talk more about Sam Harris's point of view. He believes that human morality is universal — even if we subtract God from the equation. He thinks there are objective rights and wrongs and takes offense at the "politically correct" point of view that all cultures and all societies are on equal footing in terms of what is right and what is not. Harris argues these points very eloquently, and I don't want to try to speak for him when he can do it so much better himself. Read his books if you want his opinion. I'll give you mine here.

In the novel *Brothers Karamazov* by Dostoyevsky, one of the Karamazov brothers says, "Without God, anything is permitted." Like the character in the novel, many people believe that morality comes from God and that people will only behave nicely to each other if they think God is watching. I spoke a little about this in chapter 1 when I wrote about Lance Wolf being beaten to death in Jerusalem. Buddhism doesn't frame its moral stance in terms of what will or will not get you punished by God. But it contains the belief that there is right action, and that right action is not simply a subjective thing that anyone can decide for him- or herself. One of the most important Buddhist poems, called "*Sandokai*," or "The Harmony of Difference and Equality," says, "Don't set up standards of your own." This poem is so important that in some Zen temples the monks chant it weekly to remind themselves of its message.

Yet even though the Buddhist concept of morality is that moral action is objective, it is not that moral action is always exactly the same in the superficial sense. Harris puts this in interesting terms. He says that there is a "moral landscape" with peaks and valleys, and that even though each peak does not look exactly like every other peak, we can still recognize the high points as high and the low points as low.

We desperately need to come to terms with what is and what is not moral behavior in a sense that is devoid of sectarianism. But what about when people who have to live together disagree about what is and is not moral?

When I was in Jerusalem I saw some Orthodox Jewish women wearing head coverings, as well as a number of Muslim women wearing *hijab*. The word *hijab* can refer to a wide variety of things. In one sense it simply means "modest dress." In common usage, though, it generally refers to head scarves worn by women to show their modesty. Sometimes *hijab* is taken to further extremes in the form of full-body coverings known as burkas.

I only saw three women wearing burkas during the week I spent in Jerusalem. Most of the Palestinian women I saw there didn't dress much more modestly than most Jewish women I saw. Few wore any kind of head covering at all. What was weird to me was that I had a funny reaction every time I saw a woman in Jerusalem dressed in a short skirt or hot pants or anything like that. There were almost as few women dressed that way as dressed in burkas. Whenever I saw one I was a little taken aback.

Now, normally I am not at all shocked by the sight of immodestly dressed women. In fact, quite the opposite. I spent ten years in Tokyo, where some women seem to take pride in pushing the limits of what is considered acceptable dress. Some women there appeared to be challenging the very laws of physics. This never bothered me at all. In fact, I enjoyed it.

But that was Tokyo. In Jerusalem such dress just did not seem appropriate. In fact, it seemed to represent a challenge to the culture, a kind of slap in the face to Orthodox Jews and observant Muslims alike. Maybe it was.

In Israel there are laws protecting a person's right to dress the way she wants to, within certain very broad limits. The most powerful people in that society believe that the way a person dresses is not a significant moral issue. On the other hand, murder, as in the case of Lance Wolf, is considered a significant issue. Even if some parts of Israeli society see immodest dress as offensive to God, the people in power do not. Or if they do, they don't believe it should be a legal matter. In terms of the moral landscape, murder would be a big valley, while immodest dress would be a pothole at most.

I am not averse to dressing in ways that challenge the norms of society. I was part of the punk rock movement, after all. We were all about challenging the prevailing norms of society. And some of us — not me — were not afraid to fight, quite literally, for our right to dress how we wanted. So I have a lot of sympathy for women in Jerusalem who want to shake up the Orthodox folks. I think they ought to be shaken up.

But sometimes I don't feel as punk rock as I used to. I don't think the way a person dresses is a moral issue. But some folks do. And in every society there are certain accepted norms. Sometimes those norms are dead wrong. Yet the society has agreed to them, or been forced to agree to them. I am not at all in favor of blind conformity. But sometimes conformity with eyes wide open can get you farther than flouting society's mistaken ideas will. It's always a tough call to make. When I was young, flouting the norms and freaking out the people who clung to them seemed like a good idea. Now I tend to dress and act a bit more conservatively in order to draw those people in before I hit 'em up with the hard stuff.

The question, though, is whether or not there is some underlying moral structure to human relations. Often atheists like to point out the fallacy of believing that God creates all good. If God is the source of all good, then whatever he says is good *must* be good. If God were to say that torture and murder were good, then they would be. But most of us don't believe that. And if you don't believe God can make something good by simply deciding to make it good, then you have to say that morality is above God.

Of course, plenty of people really *do* believe that God can decide that bad things are good. This is why they can blow up office buildings or buses in the name of God. Most of us, though, think those people are crazy. I certainly do.

I don't think that God is either able to bend morality according to his will or somehow subservient to a morality that is above him. I think the universal morality that Harris postulates is an example of God. God is neither above nor below morality. There is no difference between morality and God.

Nishijima Roshi often uses the phrase "Rule of the Universe" to describe his ideas about universal morality. He believes that the universe has rules. Some of these we already know about, like gravity and the conservation of energy and so on. Nishijima believes that these rules extend into the area of moral action. In fact, it's fair to say that Buddhism in general sees the laws of right moral action as inherent in the structure of the universe itself.

If you take a mechanistic view of things, that idea sounds absurd. The mechanistic view has it that what we do is pretty much arbitrary. We are bound by the laws of physics. But we are not bound by any laws of morality. That's pretty plain to see if you just look at the headlines in any newspaper anywhere in the world any day of the week.

But Buddhism doesn't see reality as mechanistic. Our subjective experience of the world is as real a thing as concrete matter. We are free to behave immorally, but there are always consequences to such action.

We can deny those consequences and pretend they don't exist, but that won't change a thing.

Stephen Batchelor rejects the Buddhist notion of karma, at least as it's understood by many today. The typical understanding of karma is that the universe keeps tabs on the good and evil that we do and metes out rewards and punishments accordingly. If there's a God or a universe that rewards good and punishes evil, then we have to deal with what philosophers call the "problem of evil."

In one of the oldest records of his sayings, Buddha brings up what we today would call the problem of evil as an argument against the existence of God. He says, "There are recluses who maintain and believe that whatever a man experiences, be it pleasant, unpleasant or neutral — all that is caused by God's act of creation. If that is so then people commit murder, theft and unchaste deeds due to God's act of creation, they indulge in lying, slanderous and harsh talk due to God's act of creation, they are covetous, hateful and hold wrong views due to God's act of creation."*

In *The Jataka Tales*, the stories of Buddha's supposed previous existences, the problem of evil comes up again. Buddha says there, "If Brahma is the lord and creator of the whole world why has he not made the entire world happy without ordaining misfortune in the world? Why has he made the world full of injustice, deceit, falsehood and conceit? The lord of beings, then, is evil, since he has ordained unrighteousness when there could have been righteousness."†

Buddhists by and large do not believe in a God who watches over us, rewarding our virtuous deeds and punishing our sinful ones. However, we do talk about karma, an idea that is widely misunderstood in the West. Some who hear about karma equate it with a watchful God doling out rewards and punishments, only without invoking the idea of

---

* From *Early Buddhism and the Bhagavad Gita* by Motilal Banarsidass.
† From *Early Buddhism*.

God. But it's not the same thing at all. Some say that we must believe in God or at least in karma, or society will fall apart.

For example, the guys who killed Lance Wolf were at least nominally Muslim. But they did not have a real belief in God. Because if they believed that Allah saw all their actions, they would have feared reprisals for beating up a scrawny guy in a back alley.

Fear of God is supposed to be more potent than fear of the law. If you beat up a scrawny guy in a back alley in the middle of the night the law might not catch you. But God is the ultimate security camera. He sees everything. So God will definitely catch you and punish you, and that punishment will be more severe than anything the law can come up with.

One important societal function of faith in God, then, is to keep order. I've long felt that phrases like "the fear of God is the beginning of wisdom" (Proverbs 9:10) were meant to convey this sense of God. The fear that you will be punished by God for acting immorally is the beginning of the wisdom of learning to act morally.

Of course, this function of God doesn't always work out the way it should, even when people have faith. It's easy enough for a religious leader to convince people that in certain cases God wants them to do some maiming and killing. Still, even in these cases, God is seen as protecting good people from evil.

An unspoken idea has been circulating for thousands of years that if you don't believe in God you're a danger to society. There was probably a time in many emerging civilizations when anyone who didn't believe in the prevailing religion actually *was* dangerous to society. To say you didn't believe in God in those days was like saying today that you don't believe in the laws of your nation. Protecting religion and forcing it on those who may not have wanted it was a way of ensuring that society could continue to exist and function, the same way we contemporary people force anyone who might not care for speed limits to follow them anyway.

Forcing unbelievers to submit to the prevailing belief in God was a way of preserving social order. The view that preserving religious belief is the way to preserve social order has been passed down without most of us realizing its original function. This, I believe, can account for some of the almost maniacal urgency that many "true believers" have toward converting everyone to their way of thinking, even if the believers themselves don't understand why they do it.

The concept of karma can function in much the same way. But it's subtler and more rational than that. The word *karma* means "action." We know that all action in the physical world has some kind of effect. The study of cause-and-effect relationships in the physical world is the foundation of science. In a sense we could say that science is the study of certain aspects of the law of karma.

Buddhism extends the observable physical laws of cause and effect into the nonphysical realm. This makes sense based on the Buddhist proposition that form is emptiness and emptiness is form or, in other words, that matter is the immaterial and the immaterial is matter. Cause and effect is then not limited to physical reactions occurring within material substances.

I realize it's tough to believe this. We always see what appears to be immoral behavior being materially rewarded, while moral behavior goes unrewarded or is even punished. Good people die of Lou Gehrig's disease. Bad people get rich and live in mansions in the Hollywood Hills.

In the *Shobogenzo* chapter called "Karma in the Three Times," Dogen says,

Retribution for good and bad has three times. Generally, people only see that to the good [comes] early death; to the violent, long life; to the evil, fortune; and to the righteous, calamity; where-upon [people] say that there is no cause and effect and no wrong-ness or happiness. Particularly, they do not know that shadow and sound accord with [their sources], not differing by a thou-sandth or a hundredth and — even with the passing of a hundred thousand myriad *kalpas* [a *kalpa* is 4.32 billion years] — never wearing away.

But most of us won't be convinced by this argument, since it seems to require a belief in reincarnation. To be satisfied by this line of reasoning, you have to believe that evildoers who make a fortune in this life get reincarnated as worms or slugs or something as retribution. If you believe that, fine. But most of us don't. I don't. And yet I still feel that what Dogen says here makes sense and fits my real experience.

What convinced me about the law of karma was being able to see it at work in my own life. It took about ten years of daily zazen practice before I just started to barely perceive it.

This is because sometimes cause-and-effect links are not readily apparent, especially if you've got a vested interest in seeing things the wrong way. One of the most popular YouTube videos is an ad from the 1950s for Camel cigarettes that begins with a narrator asking, "What brand of cigarette do you smoke, doctor?" The aim of these ads was to fend off claims that cigarettes were bad for your health. It's hard for us now to believe it, but at the time there was some doubt as to whether smoking cigarettes was linked to lung cancer. This real doubt was coupled with a desire to continue earning the money from cigarette sales and endorsements. After a while, though, new research erased those doubts. Now very few of us question the link between smoking and cancer. Once we learn how to see cause-and-effect relationships even when we don't want to, they become so obvious we wonder how we could have missed them.

Sometimes when people hear that I believe in karma they get very upset. They start bringing up things like innocent Iraqi babies being blown up by American smart bombs or nice people like my mom getting terrible diseases. They accuse me of saying that these people somehow deserved their suffering. They say that karma is a philosophical justification for blaming the victim.

But I never think about karma in terms of other people's lives, only in terms of my own. I don't look at a homeless person and go, "That guy musta done something really awful!" Nor do I think, "Jeez, that guy Lance certainly did bad stuff in his past lives to have ended up

getting beaten to death on the streets of Jerusalem." It's not my business to make that kind of judgment. It couldn't possibly help anything,
anyway, even if I made such a judgment and even if it turned out I
was correct. If I do happen to catch myself entertaining such useless
thoughts, I ignore them.

But also when I see a supposedly "evil" person being rewarded by
society, I have to wonder if the happiness he projects is real or if the
evil I believe him to have done is truly evil. Since I can't answer either
of these questions, I have to also consign such judgments to the heap
of silly and useless thoughts, just like thoughts about blameless people
who end up victims of bad fortune. Besides, what seems to be bad fortune often is not and what looks like good fortune often turns out to
have negative effects.

However, I am able to continuously watch the careless actions that
I take meet with bad effects and the nice things I do meet with good
results. It happens all the time — so often that I would feel foolish
denying it. So I accept it. And I try to be careful. When I slip up —
which is all the time — the universe puts me in my place.

If you haven't been able to watch this for yourself it probably just
seems like a groundless belief or wishful thinking. It might look like the
delusion some psychologists call the "just world hypothesis." *Wikipe-
dia* defines this as "the tendency for people to want to believe that the
world is fundamentally just so when they witness an otherwise inexplicable injustice they will rationalize it by searching for things that the
victim might have done to deserve it. This deflects their anxiety, and
lets them continue to believe the world is a just place, but often at the
expense of blaming victims for things that were not, objectively, their
fault."

Blaming the victims is not what Buddhism is about. Even if I
believe that cause and effect operates in all situations, in the real world
real things actually happen to real people. A Buddhist's responsibility is
to help, not to judge or place blame. In the moment things are happening, who is to blame matters very little, anyway.

Nor must you blame yourself when a seemingly unaccountable evil befalls you. You don't really know what's good for you and what's not. After I graduated from college I applied for loads of jobs in Akron, Ohio, where I lived. I got turned down for every one. At the time I moaned bitterly about the unfairness of my fate. But it was getting turned down for those jobs that led me to take the desperate action of moving to Japan. My life improved dramatically because of what I had thought to be dire circumstances. Happens all the time.

To acknowledge the role of cause and effect is not to blame anyone for anything. It would be just as ridiculous to blame a match for catching fire when struck. Our definitions of what is good fortune and what is bad fortune are mostly worthless.

As far as whether or not our good and bad deeds meet with good and bad ends, I think a lot of people today see it as a choice of three options: 1) You believe that the universe is dead matter, morality is arbitrary, and life is an accident. 2) You believe that God exists, rewards good and punishes evil, performs miracles, and is the property of one specific religion. 3) You simply do not know.

I know that many nuanced arguments lie in between these choices. But it seems that most of us think those are our only options. I know I did for a long time. And yet I now think it's not that we must choose between faith and reason, but that there's a kind of faith that can be reasonable as well, as we've talked about.

Yet the unreasonable idea of God as miracle worker persists. Let's look at that next.

CHAPTER 14

DOES GOD WORK MIRACLES IN BROOKLYN?

Winter is cold in Brooklyn. I'd been living in Los Angeles for five years before I moved to New York. In LA, the natives sometimes refer to something they call "winter." That's when you have to wear a long-sleeved T-shirt instead of a regular T-shirt. Before that I spent ten years in Tokyo, where they have a legitimate winter, but it's very mild.

In Brooklyn, though, winter is damned cold. As I typed the first draft of this chapter it was well below freezing outside. I'd been holed up in my apartment for weeks. There's a lot to see and do in the Big Apple, sure. But sometimes it's just too cold even to go outside.

One night my friend Marc invited me to his place in Brooklyn Heights to hang out and listen to records. Marc's got a real record player and plenty of groovy vinyl albums from the sixties to spin on it. He lives a couple of blocks away from the famed Brooklyn Promenade, where you can stroll along the shores of the Hudson River and take in a magnificent view of lower Manhattan and the Brooklyn Bridge.

But when we went out to the promenade I nearly froze to death in the wind. Even layered up with thermal underwear, a T-shirt, a flannel shirt, a hoodie, and my grandfather's old wool coat, plus a hat and a scarf, I was still chilled to the bone. It's been a very long time since I've experienced that kind of cold. Marc took to it like it was nothing. He's been in New York for decades.

We were out on the promenade on our way to pick up a pizza at Grimaldi's, a legendary Brooklyn Heights pizzeria. When I stepped inside the place my glasses immediately steamed up and stayed that way for about ten minutes. Our pizza was piping hot when we got it and nearly frozen solid by the time we made it back to his place, seven minutes later. Over frozen pizza the discussion got a little philosophical. Marc asked me what I was writing about, and I told him I was working on a book about the Zen concept of God. This got him very interested.

Marc was raised Catholic and had received some fairly heavy childhood indoctrination about God. So the subject was a little touchy for him. After I finished telling him that I didn't believe in God as a guy who sits outside the universe judging our sins and so on and that I believed that the nonmaterial aspects of our existence were real elements of the natural universe, and that we might call those aspects of the universe God, he relaxed. He said, "Okay. I can believe in that kind of God. I just don't believe in magic."

I think that for a lot of people God means magic. For these folks a belief in God implies a belief that there is some kind of great spirit in the sky who can alter the laws of cause and effect at will. When God is responsible for altering these laws, though, the truly faithful won't call that magic. They call it a miracle.

Some people call the birth of a baby a miracle. Others would call a truly good new movie starring Eddie Murphy a miracle. Those kinds of miracles I can believe in, or in the case of Eddie Murphy, I accept that they are possible. But when religious people talk about miracles, they're talking about something else. They're talking about Moses parting the Red Sea, or Lazarus being brought back from the dead, or a piece of toast with the face of Christ burnt into it being able to cure cold sores.

Here is how the website Christian Apologetics and Research Ministry (carm.org) defines miracles as they relate to the existence of God:

In the context of Christianity, miracles are the product and the work of God who created the natural laws as well as the universe. If someone believes that there is no God and also believes in what is called naturalism — that all things in the universe are subject to natural physical laws — then miracles are defined out of existence. On the other hand, if someone believed that there was a God and that God is involved in the world, then it is easy to acknowledge that miracles can occur.

I do believe in what these guys define as "naturalism along with its companion, evolution." I also believe in God and that God is involved in the world. So why do I believe that God cannot perform miracles?

For one thing, what I refer to as God is completely at odds with the image that lies behind the people at carm.org's argument. They believe that God is basically a person like us, only he's much, much bigger and much, much more powerful.

The standard attributes of God given by religious people are that he is wise, good, infinite, sovereign, holy, omniscient, faithful, loving, self-sufficient, self-existent, just, forgiving, immutable, merciful, eternal, gracious, omnipresent, and omnipotent. But, they say, if he can't bend the laws of cause and effect, he's not all-powerful; therefore, he's not God.

I don't really accept those attributes of God. To me, giving something an attribute suggests placing a limitation on that thing. As that Irish philosopher Eriugena said, God transcends any attributes we could imagine. Attributes, qualities, and characteristics all distinguish something from other things. But one of God's attributes is that he *is* everything. So in a sense we can say he possesses those qualities listed above. But in addition we would have to add an infinite list of other qualities, many of which would be the opposite of the standard attributes.

Ultimately this whole exercise is just a thought game and has little real value. You could argue this stuff back and forth for a thousand years and never come to any conclusion. This is, in fact, what has happened in the history of philosophy and religion. Certain people never seem to tire of these kinds of arguments. I myself tire of them very quickly.

As a Buddhist my duty is to try and come to terms with the reality that stares me in the face every single day. And in that reality the law of cause and effect is absolute and the presence of God is undeniable. I'm well aware that there are those who claim they have been eyewitnesses to events that break the laws of cause and effect. But I myself have never come across any such thing.

I can't believe the biblical accounts of miracles for the same reason I can't believe the Warren Commission's conclusions about the assassination of John F. Kennedy or even Oliver Stone's conclusions, although Stone's conclusions seem somewhat more plausible. In Kennedy's case, even with photographic documentation and a few still-living witnesses, there is still no conclusive proof. The accounts in the Bible are two thousand or more years older and backed up by far less reliable evidence. In any case, why should I trust the miracles recounted in the Bible any more than the ones in the Qur'an or the Bhagavad Gita or in any other religious scripture? Even the miracles in Buddhist scriptures strike me as unbelievable. If I need to accept all of them, that's just far too many. Especially since my own experience is that miracles in the religious sense do not occur.

As for the reliability of scripture, one scripture I do believe is the one in which Buddha says, "Don't believe in what is written in scripture." That's in the Kalama Sutra, by the way. And I don't believe it because Buddha said it. I believe it because it makes sense.

So what is God if he cannot perform miracles? As I've said, to me, life itself is God. The real concrete experience of life right at this place and right at this very moment is God. I don't have to seek evidence far away or in dubious stories about miracles in the distant past in order to believe in God.

Religious people go to great lengths to distinguish between magic and miracles. This is a matter of tremendous importance in Christianity. Even in his lifetime, Jesus was accused of performing magic. His disciples countered by saying it wasn't magic but miracles. In the disciples' belief system, as in a lot of Christian belief systems today, both magic and miracles are possible. Miracles are the work of God, and magic is the work of Satan. Yet magical acts and miraculous ones are indistinguishable. They are both instances in which the laws of cause and effect are temporarily overcome by a supernatural force.

Since they are so similar, religious people who believe in such things must be careful to clarify which is which. It used to be in the Catholic Church that a person had to have worked miracles in order to be canonized as a saint. But it was crucial to also prove that what had happened could not be attributed to magic.

During my first class about Zen Buddhism I asked the teacher if Buddha was ever reported to have performed miracles. At the time I didn't really believe in miracles, nor was it important to me to believe that Buddha could do miraculous things in order for me to have faith in his teachings. I just wanted to know if that was part of the tradition.

The teacher told me that some older scriptures could be interpreted that way. He cited one in which Buddha is supposed to have flown up into the air during one of his discourses and spun around, breathing fire. This sounded much cooler to me than any of the miracles attributed to Jesus! But, the teacher said, not many Buddhists take those stories as the literal truth.

In a good number of sutras Buddha does some pretty amazing things that could be viewed as miracles. In Zen these are usually seen as literary devices created by the sutra writers to give a sense of how monumental and deeply moving Buddha's teachings were to his audiences; they are not generally presented as evidence of Buddha's supernatural abilities. But sometimes they are. In his book *Confessions of a Buddhist Atheist* Stephen Batchelor talks about the Buddhist teachers who say that one must accept Buddha's supernatural abilities as real or the whole philosophy of Buddhism is null and void. My teachers were not like that. In fact, I don't know of any Zen teachers who would insist on such a thing.

The idea of Buddha having miraculous powers does occur in some forms of Buddhism. Some sutras claim that Buddha had certain paranormal capabilities, such as the ability to recall past lives or to know the minds of others. Since Buddha could recall all his past lives, some say, that meant he was deeply aware of the fundamental structure of the universe and therefore that his opinions about how people ought to live have more value than those of someone who cannot recall his past lives.

Dogen was not convinced by such reasoning. In a *Shobogenzo* chapter titled "The Power to Know Others' Minds" ("*Tashintsu*"), he tells the story of a mystic named Sanzo who has returned from India and claims to have attained the power to read minds. This supernatural ability impressed a lot of people and gained Sanzo many followers. The emperor asked Master Echu, known as the National Master because the emperor trusted him as his personal Buddhist teacher, to examine Sanzo.

Echu said, "I hear you have the power to know others' minds."

Sanzo said, "I would not be so bold as to say so." This is a typical response intended to convey a degree of humility. But we can be certain that *someone* was spreading the idea that Sanzo could read minds. Probably Sanzo was clever enough to obscure his own part in spreading the rumor. Lots of spiritual masters these days do pretty much the same thing, allowing their fans to spread wild rumors of their powers and then playing coy when questioned about them — but back to our story.

Echu said, "Tell me where this old monk is right now."

Sanzo said, "Master, you are the teacher of the whole country. Why have you gone to the West River to watch a boat race?"

Echu said, "Tell me where this old monk is now."

Sanzo said, "Master, you are the teacher of the whole country. Why are you on a bridge watching someone play with a monkey?"

Echu said, "Tell me where this old monk is now."

Sanzo went quiet for a while. Finally he gave up.

Echu said, "You ghost of a wild fox! Where is your power to know others' minds?"

The common understanding of this story is that Echu was thinking about certain situations the first two times and that Sanzo read his mind correctly. The final time, though, Echu entered into some kind of state of nonthinking and Sanzo couldn't read anything.

According to Dogen, all commentators assume that Sanzo got it right the first two times. But Dogen says that Sanzo gave the wrong answer every time. According to Dogen the real meaning of Echu's question "Where is this old monk now?" is "Just what kind of moment is this one?" This question, Dogen says, asserts that "this is the place where something ineffable exists." It points to the ultimate inexpressibility of things just as they are.

In other words, Echu is not asking Sanzo to read his mind when he asks Sanzo to say where he is. He is asking Sanzo to tell him where the man who actually stands in front of him is right now. He wants Sanzo to tell him what this real world is.

Dogen says that Echu is not necessarily an old monk "but [that] an old monk is always a fist." He means that the self Echu expressed as an old monk is always present. The self that was expressed as an old monk in the case of Echu is the same self that is expressed as you read this book right now.

Dogen isn't impressed by Sanzo's ability. He says that what common people call the power to know others' minds is just the power to know the images in other people's heads. Mind readers, he says, may be able to dimly detect, on the outer reaches of perception, the images arising in the minds of others. But this power doesn't mean anything in terms of understanding the truth that Buddhism is trying to get at. "The mind is not always mental images," he says, "and mental images are not always the mind."

Dogen then goes on at length about how powers such as mind reading, even if they exist, have no bearing on Buddhist understanding. That someone possesses such an ability does not indicate that he has anything valuable to teach us about the underlying nature of reality. In the *Shobogenzo* chapter titled "Deep Belief in Cause and Effect" ("*Shin*

Jin Inga," in Japanese), Dogen relates the story of a monk who could supposedly remember five hundred previous lifetimes. About this Dogen says, "There are those among human beings, or among other beings, who innately possess the power to see a while back into former states. But it is not the seed of clear understanding: it is an effect felt from bad conduct. Even knowing a thousand lives or ten thousand lives does not always produce the Buddha's teaching." By "bad conduct" he is referring to what some folks today would call "bad karma." To Dogen so-called supernatural abilities were a liability to be overcome, not a special talent to be lauded.

Dogen's attitude about supernatural powers is similar to the one expressed by the late British author Christopher Hitchens, who was willing to concede that perhaps Jesus was born of a virgin, performed miracles, and rose from the dead. But even if all these things were true, it still would not prove to him that what Jesus said was valid. I have to agree. It's like when people put a lot of stock in what famous actors have to say. Just because someone is rich and talented doesn't mean she has the answers to everything. Nor would someone's ability to walk on water mean she knew the deepest truths about the universe.

I believe it's quite possible that there are levels of perception available to those who practice detecting them that are not available to most people. I feel I've come into contact with a certain degree of this kind of thing during the course of my practice. Funny things seem to happen during Zen retreats, wherein the barriers between people dissolve in unusual ways. I've also had conversations with my Zen teachers in which we seemed to engage in an uncommon level of nonverbal communication. People in love can sometimes communicate with each other in inexplicable ways. This is nothing miraculous. It only indicates that we function on levels we generally tend to ignore.

As for events that bend the laws of nature, Dogen was quite adamant that Buddhists should never accept such ideas. He expresses his condemnation of the idea of miracles and magic most clearly in the *Shobogenzo* chapter "Deep Belief in Cause and Effect" referred to a few

paragraphs ago. This is a key part of Dogen's teaching. In fact, one of
the most popular souvenirs at the Tassajara Zen Monastery gift shop
(yes, there's a gift shop) is a shirt that says *Shinjin Inga* in Chinese
characters. When they first had the shirts printed one of the Chinese
characters was wrong and they had to send them all back. Such are the
ways of cause and effect!

In this chapter Dogen quotes the ancient Buddhist master Nagarjuna as saying, "If we deny the existence of cause and effect in the world,
as do people of non-Buddhism, then there is no present or future; and
if we deny the existence of cause and effect beyond the world, then
there are no Three Treasures, Four Noble Truths, or four effects of a
sramana." The Three Treasures are the cornerstones of Buddhist life:
Buddha himself, his teachings (the dharma), and the Buddhist community (the sangha). The Four Noble Truths are the major truths on
which Buddhism is based. A *sramana* is a person who renounces the
world and is supposed to gain benefits by doing so.

Furthermore, Dogen says, "[Some say] spiritual essence is just the
mind, for the mind is not the same as the body. Such understanding is
just non-Buddhism. Some say that when human beings die, they unfail-
ingly return to the ocean of spiritual essence. Even if they do not practice and learn the Buddha-Dharma, they will naturally return to the
ocean of enlightenment, whereupon the wheel of life and death will
turn no more. For this reason, there will be no future. This is the nihil-
istic view of non-Buddhism."

A lot of people these days are very fond of the Buddhist idea that
the present moment is the only true reality. But they misconstrue this
as a belief that the past and the future don't exist. In one sense they
don't exist, in that they don't exist somewhere else. There isn't a past
or a future into which we can travel the way we can travel to, say, New
York or Saskatoon. But the past and the future do exist. They exist right
here, right now. We are the expression of our past, and our actions now
create our future. Past and future are intimately present with us at this
real moment.

The denial of cause and effect allows us to believe in miracles and magic. But in Buddhism there are no miracles, and there is no magic. Granted, there may be aspects of cause and effect that we do not fully understand. If someone could cleverly manipulate those aspects, she would appear capable of miracles. But such a person would be no more capable of actual miracles than the Spaniards who frightened the Native Americans with the "magic" of gunpowder. A mind reader like Sanzo might be such a person, no worthier of worship than those Spanish conquistadors.

During a Brooklyn winter the only real miracle would be something that would make the temperature tolerable. But perhaps that's already happened. We were nice and warm in Marc's apartment listening to old Yardbirds albums and rare records by the Fuzztones and Plan Nine. Maybe that's all the miracle we need.

CHAPTER 15

GOD DOESN'T HAVE
TO BE REAL TO EXIST

Every morning for the past month or so, right after I finish my morning zazen, I've been following a little ritual. I light a stick of incense, do three full-body prostrations, and recite the Heart Sutra.* I do not do this because I think Buddha or God is up there listening to me and needs to be reminded that I think he's supercool. I don't do it because I think bad things might happen to me if I fail to. I don't even do it because I'm with a bunch of other people who do it and I worry that I might be ostracized if I don't. No one else is there except for Crum the Cat, who usually sits and watches me. He must think I'm weird. Anyway, the reason I do it is because it feels real good.

When I was in Tassajara, Greg Fain, the practice leader, insisted that I perform the traditional role of a Zen priest and lead some of the rituals. I really didn't want to. And I probably could have talked my way out of it. But I decided it wouldn't be a bad thing to do.

In addition to leading some of the ceremonies, I was required to participate in a morning service each day at dawn. This consisted of nine full-body prostrations, group recitation of the Heart Sutra, group recitation of the names of great Buddhist masters of the past — both

---

* A full-body prostration is a really big bow, in which you go all the way down on your knees and bend your neck till your head touches the floor.

male and female — more bows, and finally group recitation of one of a revolving group of sutras that changed each day, followed by a few more bows for good measure. And you know what? That felt great too.

In his book *Religion for Atheists*, Alain de Botton argues that atheists can learn a lot from religion. He says that religious institutions are generally better at educating their members about what they feel are important truths than are nonreligious educational institutions. Religions have special days each year when certain significant matters are supposed to be commemorated. They also have rituals in which the major tenets of their creed are repeated daily. Religions involve both the mind and body by integrating their insights with physical practices like baptism or the Buddhist tea ceremony. Religions form communities that support each other in ways that secular communities often fail to. Religious people create works of art intended to express their philosophies. Mr. de Botton asks if we can't create atheistic versions of these same kinds of things.

I would argue that Zen Buddhism already has what most atheists would define as atheistic versions of some of these same things — that is, if those atheists took the time to look closely into what Zen really teaches rather than immediately dismissing it as a religion and therefore not worth the trouble. Be that as it may, I'm not sure we really can create a perfectly secular version for every aspect of education without ending up with something like Nazism or Soviet-style communism. And we all know how well those worked out. I have, however, seen some stuff that makes me think that something a bit like what Mr. de Botton proposes could work, at least on a smaller scale.

In July 2011 Zero Defex, the hardcore punk band I play bass in, got invited to play at a festival called X-Day held in the Wisteria campgrounds near the southeast Ohio town of Pomeroy. There were naked people all over the place. I watched a guy play baseball using a Ping-Pong ball for a ball and his dick for a bat. There were drum circles and people in tie-dyed shirts. There were pagans and Wiccans and Rastafarians galore. I think there might even have been a bit of illegal drug usage.

X-Day is an annual festival held by the Church of the SubGenius. The Church of the SubGenius was founded by a Cleveland-based artist who calls himself the Reverend Ivan Stang. I stayed in a house just outside the campgrounds with the reverend and his significant other, Connie, for a couple of nights while I was there.

The reverend told me that he started his church basically as a joke. Sometime in the seventies he began making fake religious tracts. He'd Xerox these and put them in the kinds of random places you often find real religious tracts lying around in — Laundromats, bookstores, bus stops. The reverend's sister-in-law was in the publishing business and insisted that there was potential for a book based on these fake religious tracts. An editor at McGraw-Hill books agreed. He got in touch with Rev. Stang, and they put together *The Book of the SubGenius*.

The book is full of wonderful weirdness. There are yetis and UFOs and the ubiquitous J. R. "Bob" Dobbs, a pipe-smoking white man seemingly designed by a fifties ad agency whom the then-nonexistent Church of the SubGenius regarded as its prophet. The book became a big hit and is still in print after more than thirty years.

But Rev. Stang had a problem. Although the book was so over the top you'd think that no one could ever miss the fact that it was a joke, Rev. Stang says, "You wouldn't believe how many people wanted to take that shit seriously!" Rev. Stang put out a follow-up in which he tried to make it even clearer that the whole thing was a big joke. Yet even then certain people still believed. "If I learned to keep a straight face I could be making more money than the Scientologists," he says.

One of the more blatantly absurd statements Rev. Stang made was that on July 5, 1998, an army of aliens would arrive on Earth to whisk the loyal members of his church away in their pleasure saucers and wipe out the nonbelievers. A big party was held on that day, and when the saucers failed to arrive, the Rev. Stang cited a number of outlandish conspiracy theories to explain why they hadn't come. He said they would surely show up next July 5. Every year since, the SubGeniuses have gathered on July 5 to await the aliens, and every year the reverend comes up with new excuses for why they didn't show up.

It's basically just a big party in the woods, and although there may be a few believers in the crowd, most folks seem to get that it's a joke. Yet they still play along, giving rousing sermons laced with SubGenius buzzwords and engaging in the bizarre rites and rituals of the church, like a baptism where your old sins are washed away and you receive new ones in return. Yet somehow, this fake church also does a lot of people a lot of good.

A couple of hours before Zero Defex took the stage I met a woman who called herself Susie the Floozy. Susie the Floozy has a condition called prosopagnosia that renders her unable to recognize people's faces. She told me that if she saw me later that day she'd probably know who I was, but that if we were to meet again in a week she'd have no idea who I was and would probably introduce herself all over again. I kinda feel like I have the same problem sometimes.

Susie the Floozy also told me that the Church of the SubGenius saved her life. At one point her condition, as well as a number of other factors in her life, had her convinced that she might as well just end it all. But then she came across *The Book of the SubGenius*, and it offered her direction and a kind of peace. She knew the whole thing was a put-on. But that didn't matter. She knew that whoever made it understood something profound. Eventually she hooked up with other members of the church, who took her in and accepted her. Just like a real church, the Church of the SubGenius gave Susie the Floozy a community and a sense of belonging. She found a reason to live.

I found the Church of the SubGenius's approach to their own teachings to be remarkably similar to the Mahayana Buddhist take on some of its scriptures. Mahayana means "great vehicle." It refers to a group of Buddhist sects that emerged several hundred years after Buddha died. They often developed their own brand-new sutras that followed the forms of the old ones, such as the Lotus Sutra, which we looked at earlier. They put lots of new words into the mouths of historical figures like Shakyamuni Buddha and his disciples, who had been dead for ages.

We know full well that sutras like the Lotus Sutra, the Lankavatara Sutra, and even the Heart Sutra are in some sense false in that they claim to contain the words of the Buddha and his immediate disciples but were composed hundreds of years after all those people were dead. Yet in spite of the lies contained within them, these sutras are essentially true because they express something profoundly real.

This is why religious people who insist on the supposed "literal truth" of their scriptures have got it all wrong. Scriptures don't need to be literally true to have deep meaning, the same way that novels and poems don't need to be literally true in order to affect us.

It doesn't matter if the stuff recorded in the Bible "literally" happened or not, as long as the messages those stories are intended to convey are true. This whole obsession with the literal truth of scripture is ruining a lot of the good that people might otherwise be able to find in their religions.

This idea of the Bible as literal truth is very much an American phenomenon. But it has spread to other parts of the world, just like many other aspects of American culture. And it's a silly idea because most of those who espouse it don't even believe it themselves.

Maybe they believe the Earth was created in six days, that there was a big flood, and that Jesus rose from the dead. But few of them believe that the Earth is flat and held up by big pillars, as it says in 1 Samuel 2:8: "The pillars of the earth are the Lord's, and he hath set the world upon them." Nor are they likely to take Jesus literally when he says in Matthew 5:30, "And if thy right hand offend thee, cut it off, and cast it from thee." Although Leviticus 11 says, "Whatsoever hath no fins nor scales in the waters, that shall be an abomination unto you," they still like their fried shrimp. So it's a kind of selective literalism. Why not be more like how the members of the Church of the SubGenius are about their book and admit there's a lot of stuff in the Bible you can't possibly take literally but that it contains some important truths anyway?

Since you are reading a book called *There Is No God and He Is Always with You*, you are probably not a biblical literalist. But I think this stuff is worth mentioning because sometimes people try to force the concept of biblical literalism onto Buddhism. Here's an email I got a while ago:

> I studied the Nishijima/Cross translation of *Shobogenzo* quite a few years ago. Master Nishijima's attitude toward rebirth/reincarnation is essentially the same as I hold. However, I took and take objection to his persistent opinion that the teaching of literal rebirth is not Buddhist. I have studied Dogen quite a lot and must come to the conclusion that for Dogen literal rebirth is clearly part of his Buddhist view (it has nothing to do with the Senika view of eternalism). Like I said, my own opinion about this matter is essentially the same as Master Nishijima's but that view should not be forced upon Dogen; it is not appropriate and I feel that Master Nishijima does exactly that. When reading Dogen we should try to think like an ancient Japanese monk who viewed the world in a Mahayana Buddhist way and take what we can from it in our modern world without trying to alter aspects of it that seem alien or even superstitious to us.
>
> Anyway, Master Nishijima's persistence on this view somehow put me off his *Shobogenzo*. It has been years since I have studied his version of the *Shobogenzo* and I feel I would like to own it again so I was really excited about the Kazuaki Tanahashi's version until I read your blog. The same things that bother you about this translation would bother me too! So I'm considering buying the Nishijima version again instead. It has been so long since I have studied it so, my real question is: Does the Nishijima version sneak in some of his what I feel are modern views about rebirth/reincarnation, or is the text as literal as possible and reflect Dogen's teachings purely?

This is my reply:

> Nishijima Roshi leaves all of Dogen's references to rebirth within *Shobogenzo* just as they are in the original. People are getting reborn all over the place in that book! When people questioned Nishijima about this during talks, he always explained that these references were meant metaphorically, not literally. However, within the text of his translation he never alters any of these references, nor does he even add any footnotes saying they are metaphorical.

To me, the more direct questions are 1) "What do we today mean by 'literal rebirth'?" and 2) "Why does it matter if Dogen believed in it or not?" In the case of the questioner, the answer to #2 is he wants to know if Nishijima's translation is reliable. The answer to that is, yes, it is. So is Kaz Tanahashi's fine translation.

But I think for most people #2 is important because we regard Dogen as a religious authority. If Dogen agrees with other religious authorities, like Deepak Chopra, for example, on the question of literal rebirth, we can feel that much more relieved. As Mr. Chopra has learned, people will pay good money to be told by a religious authority figure that they will live forever. People have paid damn good money to hear that from religious authority figures for a very long time, and in cultures across the globe. It is quite a reliable strategy for making a living.

But Deepak Chopra doesn't know anything more about life after death than you do, dear reader. Dogen didn't know anything more about life after death when he was alive and writing than you do, either. I also do not know anything more than you. Unlike the "she" in John Lennon's song "She Said, She Said," I do not know what it's like to be dead.*

---

* "She" was actually Peter Fonda, out of his mind on LSD, who said this to Lennon while they were tripping together in the Hollywood Hills. I was once in line at Ralph's grocery store in West Hollywood with Peter Fonda, and he was very much alive. But after *Ghost Rider* his career was dead. Perhaps that's what he meant?

I don't necessarily think that Mr. Chopra is cynically exploiting his readers by telling them lies. I think he says what he says to create a reassuring feedback loop from himself to his readership and back again that helps relieve his own fears of death. This is also a time-tested strategy.

But back to question #1. What do we mean today by "literal rebirth"?

A now defunct website called e-sangha said this about me in reference to the above: "Brad Warner is a materialist; i.e., he denies rebirth; and therefore, the only conclusion he can assert is that the mind is merely an epiphenomenon of brain activity. That is principally why knowledgeable Buddhists take issue with him. That being so, he isn't teaching Buddhism, but instead teaching a Worldly dharma that he and his teacher call 'Zen'." Further down in the same post someone adds, "Rebirth is literal in all Buddhist traditions. It is not a metaphor, analogy, simile, or metonymy."

For starters, I have never asserted that "mind is merely an epiphenomenon of brain activity" because I didn't even know what the word *epiphenomenon* meant until I looked it up (it means a "secondary phenomenon"). But I believe that the e-sangha guy is saying that I think that the immaterial something he calls "mind" is just the activity of the material brain. In one sense that is true. But I also think that the material brain is an expression of the activity of the immaterial thing we call mind. Both material brain and immaterial mind are manifestations of something underlying them that is neither material nor immaterial but transcends any distinctions of mind and matter. I do not consider myself a materialist at all.

That's beside the point. The e-sangha guys believed in literal rebirth, and for them it was very important that others believed in it too. If they thought someone who claimed to be Buddhist denied literal rebirth, they labeled them non-Buddhist and tried to cast doubt on them by using phrases like "that is principally why knowledgeable Buddhists take issue with him." There is no evidence I am aware of that any knowledgeable Buddhists (whoever they might be) take issue with me about my stance on rebirth. It's good to be careful of vague, unattributed claims like this in general, by the way.

But still what in heck's name is literal rebirth? When you come right down to it, I suppose it means, to most people, that someone is telling them they'll live forever. Literal rebirth means that someday I will actually die as a person in some place, and I will get reborn in another place as another person, celestial being, or animal.

This is not what Buddhism teaches. Well, it's not what the kind of Buddhism I teach teaches, anyway. There is no "literal you" to get "literally reborn." And this is the heart of the argument. Dogen is pretty clear that there is no literal you. So the idea that he taught anything like what most people in the Western world mean when they use the phrase *literal rebirth* is absurd.

Since we're back on the subject of life after death, let me tell you about the time I encountered a ghost at a Zen monastery and what it means to me in terms of the afterlife.

CHAPTER 16

SUICIDE AT A ZEN MONASTERY

My friend David Coady committed suicide on July 20, 2011, at the San Francisco Zen Center. He was a monk there.

I met David for the first time about three years ago when I went to Tassajara. I was in the dining room sitting with several people I didn't know, one of whom was David. Almost immediately he and I became engaged in a conversation about how useless our Zen experience would be on a résumé. It was a funny conversation and very real. I liked David right away.

I probably hung out with David on fewer than five occasions. But I felt something deeper with him than I do with many people I see a lot more often.

Once during another visit to Tassajara I was walking around breaking the rule of not singing at the monastery by quietly singing the chorus to a Bob Dylan song called "Odds and Ends." It's from his *Basement Tapes* album. The final line of the chorus is "lost time will not be found again." That is certainly and very sadly true of the time I spent with David.

That Dylan line reminded me of the poem that's carved into all of the *hans* at Tassajara. A *han* is a board that's struck with a wooden mallet to call people to zazen or other events. On each *han* at Tassajara is written a different translation of the following Chinese poem:

Great is the matter of birth and death
Life slips quickly by
To waste time is a great shame
Time waits for no one.

David immediately recognized what I was singing and told me that he was a great fan of Dylan. He said that before he moved to Tassajara he'd had a massive collection of CDs. The only ones he'd brought with him were a set of bootlegs of rare Dylan recordings, many from the same sessions that produced the *Basement Tapes* album. He asked if I wanted to copy them. The copies of those files are still on the computer I'm using to write this book.

A year later a fire swept through the valley in which Tassajara is located.* Five monks stayed behind and saved most of the monastery from burning. Thanks to their brave efforts, only a couple of structures burned. One of those was David's cabin. All his Bob Dylan CDs melted into goo.

Sometime before the fires swept through Tassajara, David was relocated to the San Francisco Zen Center's main branch in San Francisco's Lower Haight district. It was a big change from the open isolated space of the monastery to the crowded urban temple, and David attempted suicide pretty shortly after moving there. He failed that time. He tried to kill himself by drinking hemlock tea! Who did he think he was? Socrates? I didn't see David more than a few times after his suicide attempt. One of those times the subject of his attempt came up, and we swiftly moved on to other topics. He seemed deeply embarrassed by it.

David Coady should have gone on the road with a stand-up act. When I told him that, he said he heard that a lot. He said he didn't feel he had it in him to talk in front of people. But he was naturally funny and always poignantly so. Adding to the effect was the fact that he talked in a really heavy Boston accent.

---

* There's a book about it called *Fire Monks*.

I'm very sad that he's gone.

Suicide is considered by most Christians to be a sin against God. Although Buddhists don't believe in sin, suicide is considered by most Buddhists to be a violation of the ethical precepts. The ancient Buddhist monastic rules forbid monks to kill themselves except in extraordinary circumstances, like terminal illness. But David was not terminally ill, unless one counts suicidal depression as a terminal illness. (I do not.)

Here's what I believe when it comes to suicide. Your life isn't really your own to do with as you please. That's an ego-based fallacy. You are intimately connected to every person and thing you come into contact with. You do not end at the borders of your body. You are not your own possession to throw away at will.

Sometimes people imagine they can terminate their suffering by killing themselves. I don't believe that. The idea that committing suicide will end your suffering comes from the belief that you and the world in which you live are two different things. You believe that you can leave this world and thereby leave suffering behind. But my sense, after years of zazen practice, is that this is not true. I've spent a long time watching the boundary line between what I call "me" and what I call "the rest of the world" blur and fade.

So what I'm saying here goes a little further than just the old the-show-must-go-on type thing, wherein people say you have a responsibility to your friends and family not to go off and blow your brains out in the greenhouse. I would add that you also have a responsibility to yourself and even to the universe as a whole not to do that. If you kill yourself, the suffering you thought was yours alone spreads out like a wave to those parts of the universe you've been taught to think of as separate from you. And they really aren't. They're you too.

Most people seem to feel that, if nothing else, suicide at least helps the person who does it escape the pain of life into complete oblivion. But I don't think that's true, either.

I don't base this belief on received wisdom from others or on beliefs handed down to me. I don't base it on speculating about what is most likely to happen to one who commits suicide. I base my belief on my own real experiences. In my deeper and more connected moments I've seen that there really is no oblivion into which I might escape.

The ancient Buddhist philosopher Nagarjuna said that the true basis for human life is action. We usually think that we are beings who take action. But Nagarjuna said that it is better to conceive of action as the more fundamental aspect of our being. It's not that we are creatures that take action. Rather we, as creatures, are the physical manifestations of action itself. This is a topsy-turvy way of looking at things, compared to the understanding most of us have grown up with.

About a month after David killed himself I went to Tassajara to work for part of the summer, just as I had that time when I gave the speech about Dogen's concept of God. This was about a year after I gave that speech. Everyone who knew him said that David was happiest at Tassajara. For all its hardships, he loved the place.

During this visit I was again assigned to lead some of the temple services. It's a job I hate because I never really learned all the dance moves a Zen priest needs to know to lead services. I can kind of fake my way through it. But it's blatantly obvious I don't know what I'm doing.

The first day I was scheduled to do this was hot as the dickens and I was dressed in black robes with a brown sash called a *kesa* over it. It's kind of like wearing a burka with a blanket over it. The only advantage this outfit has over a burka is that your head is left uncovered. As the priest who leads the ceremony I had to meet my attendant at a nearby building ten minutes before the service. I was nervous about being on time for the thing, so I arrived about fifteen minutes early and had to stand around under a small tree that offered precious little shade.

As I stood there alone, a strange thing happened. All at once I felt David's presence. It's hard to explain. But have you ever noticed the feeling you get when you're sitting next to a close friend or lover without speaking or even really looking at the person? You just kind of sense the person near you. That's what it felt like. It wasn't like I was thinking of him or remembering him. In fact, I was only thinking about what I had to do once I got inside and all eyes were upon me. I just felt David there. The feeling persisted for about a minute, and then it was gone.

I don't believe in ghosts. I didn't then, and I don't now. But somehow David was there. I don't want to offer any explanations for what happened that day because any I could give would sound incredibly dumb. In fact, I'm more likely in hindsight to doubt my own experience since it falls so far outside my belief system than I am to try and explain it. But it happened.

Belief in God almost always seems tied up with belief in life after death. Buddha's answer to questions about life after death was, "The question does not fit the case." Life and death don't work the way we commonly think they do. To ask whether you live on after your body dies is the wrong question entirely. The more correct and pertinent question is "What is this life I am living right now?"

The answer will not be an explanation, because no explanation could possibly encompass the totality of just this simple moment. Our intellect cuts us off from experiencing all that reality has to offer. Its job is to divide reality into neat little packages that it can manipulate.

So is David Coady still alive and haunting Tassajara even after offing himself in his bedroom? The question doesn't fit the case.

Lots of people think the question "What happens after you die?" is one of the most urgent in all philosophy. So they invent concepts like rebirth and reincarnation to try and deal with their anxiety over it. But the problem is that the question makes no sense. It doesn't fit the case, as Buddha said.

Reflecting on my meeting with David Coady now, a couple of years afterward, it's difficult to know quite what happened that day. He's not the only dead person I've encountered under similarly vague circumstances. I've run into my mom on a couple of occasions too.

Suzuki Roshi once told one of his students who was expressing a deep fear of dying, "You will always exist in the universe in one form or another." I think he was right. He was also very wise to leave it there. In the end, there isn't a whole lot else you can say.

Contemporary physics tells us that nothing is ever created or destroyed. We tend to imagine this only refers to physical substances. But, as I've already said, in Buddhism we look at the physical world and the mental or spiritual world as expressions of one unified thing that is neither matter nor spirit. So nothing spiritual is ever destroyed either. It just changes form, like material substances do.

David Coady has changed his form too. His body was cremated, and I helped his mom and his brother Stephen scatter his ashes over the hills at Tassajara on the one-year anniversary of his passing. It was another crazy-hot day in the valley, just like the day when I first met David. I was sweating like a maniac in my black robes as I accompanied the family as well as San Francisco Zen Center's abbot Steve Stückey and a few of David's friends up the steep trail leading to the stones marking the final resting places of Suzuki and Katagiri Roshi.

We walked up the hill in a stately procession led by one monk with a bell she rang every few steps and followed by another monk who rang a bell in answer to that one. It was tough not to trip on the narrow, winding path and to keep our robes from getting snagged on the bushes that line the trail.

Once we reached the top, we each said a few words about what David had meant to us. I didn't talk about my meeting with him. It seemed like too much to say just then. After we said our pieces, we climbed up to a place they call the Hog Back, from which you could see the whole of Tassajara, and tossed David's earthly remains into the wind. I told Stephen about my encounter with David the previous summer as we walked back down the hill, avoiding the poison oak that lined the trail. Stephen said that he too had run into David since his passing. But, like me, he didn't know quite what to make of those encounters.

In a very real sense, the David Coady I knew is gone and will not return. But I don't know exactly what David really was because what David really was remains forever beyond my ability to ever completely know. And in another very real sense, he's still right here with me.

CHAPTER 17

A BUDDHIST CHRISTMAS
IN MEXICO

A few years ago my dad decided he wanted to retire in Mexico. He'd been living in Texas since the early eighties, and Mexico was close by. He liked the climate and the people and the food. But most of all, Mexico is far cheaper than the United States. He figured his meager savings would last a lot longer down there. He'd just have to brush up on his Spanish.

I've taken several trips with my dad (and my mom when she was alive) to Mexico to look at places my dad thought might be nice to live in. I've been to Valladolid and Mérida in the Yucatán, I've been to Guadalajara and its suburbs, I've been to Puerto Vallarta and seen drunken American tourist girls undressing in their hotel windows, and a year and a half ago I spent Christmas in the city of Santiago de Querétaro.*

They do Christmas differently down there. In the Plaza Zenea in the town square they had a papier-mâché display of various biblical events. They had a little Garden of Eden with happy animals and Adam and Eve with big ol' fig leaves covering the naughty bits. Among the animals was a giant stuffed gorilla with big googly Ping-Pong ball eyes staring at passersby.

---

* Most people drop the "Santiago de" part.

Next to that was a display representing hell — very cool. There were bright red papier-mâché devils popping up out of the ground sporting pitchforks and horns and bat wings with little papier-mâché flames around them and red lights shining down to enhance the effect. Some of the devils were feasting on what might have been human limbs. Or maybe they were turkey legs. It was hard to tell. The hell display got a lot more traffic than the Eden display.

One night there was a huge Christmas parade with floats depicting various scenes from the Bible. They had "El Triunfo de Judith," "El Sacrificio de Isaac," "El Becerro de Oro" (the Golden Calf — I had to look that one up), and many more. They also had booths where you could get your picture taken with the Three Wise Men or Santa Claus, portrayed by costumed performers. There was plenty of cotton candy and popcorn for the kids. The little shops that sold T-shirts, souvenir trinkets, and bootleg DVDs were doing a brisk business.

I like Christmas. It could be what my friend calls the "collective effervescence" of the season. Or maybe it's the music. I confess, I really like all those goofy Christmas songs. I have a lot of alternative-type friends who hate Christmas music, seemingly just because everyone else enjoys it. But I don't hate it at all. My friends in Akron have a band called Missile Toe that plays rock-and-roll versions of Christmas songs. Very cool.

I stopped by a Catholic church near the Plaza de Armas with my dad, and we peeked in on a Mass. I couldn't understand much of what was happening. The Mass was in Spanish, which always sounds a lot holier, somehow, than English.* It's impossible for me to imagine exactly what the rituals and whatnot mean to those who participate in them. As a kid I remember feeling a little left out when my Catholic friends, the Kashingakis in Nairobi, Kenya, used to get to do all those cool rituals and I didn't.

---

* Though for all the Spanish I know it could have been in Latin pronounced with a Mexican accent.

It seems we human beings need ceremonies to keep us happy and contented. The Church of the SubGenius offers rituals to those who can't buy into the standard religious dogma but enjoy doing them anyway. Zen does too. I like the Zen way of dealing with rituals by doing them but not really believing in them. I once witnessed a solemn ceremony at Tassajara that ended up being a train wreck when several people forgot what they were supposed to do. Afterward, Leslie James, the guiding teacher said, "That's all right. It shouldn't be too perfect." This seems like the proper way to deal with religious rituals.

Mexico is a very religious country. Or at least it's a country in which the outward displays of one's faith in God are highly valued. The boardinghouse where my dad and I stayed was decorated with crosses everywhere. The taxi drivers all seem to have pictures of Jesus on their dashboards. Both the friendly guy who drove us to the local Walmart (not my idea!) at a normal pace and the surly guy who drove us back to town like a deranged maniac had pictures of Jesus on their dashboards. Though I'm certain there are Mexican atheists, it's hard to imagine that too many people in Mexico would casually deny the existence of God the way so many north of the border do.

There isn't a whole lot of Buddhism in evidence in Mexico. A few Zen groups are listed on a website called Zen in Mexico. But from what I can gather, the majority of (the small number of) Buddhists in the country practice the Tibetan version of Buddhism.

This makes sense because Mexico is mostly Roman Catholic, and Tibetan-style Buddhism has a lot of rituals and costuming that are similar to those of Catholicism. In fact, one very early European traveler said that Satan had infected Tibet with his own evil corruption of Catholicism. Whatever.

I heard a story while I was in Mexico that I think says a lot, not just about Mexico but about Buddhism in the West as well. The person who told me the story didn't know if it actually happened. But he thought it might have. Apparently sometime a century or two ago there was a big parade in a Mexican city honoring the Catholic faith. It was probably a lot like the Christmas parade I watched.

The centerpiece of the procession was a giant statue of the Virgin Mary that was to be placed in the town square. The statue was being pulled along in a cart while the crowds cheered. But then the cart hit a rock in the street and the statue toppled over. It broke open, and inside was a statue of a Mexican god from the precolonial days.

The moral of the story, as it was told to me, is that even though the Mexicans appear to be Roman Catholic, they're really following a much older tradition. The Catholic icons are merely stand-ins for the gods they worshipped before the Spaniards came and forced them to convert.

This is really an instructive story because it seems to me that followers of Buddhism in the West are often doing exactly the same thing, even if they don't realize it. We use all the buzzwords we've received from translations of Buddhist works as stand-ins for the Judeo-Christian concepts we grew up with.

It's impossible to translate the literature of one culture into the language of another without doing at least a little of this. When Buddhism was first imported from India to China, a lot of the words of the native Chinese Taoist philosophy were pressed into service to stand in for Buddhist concepts. When you read Buddhist texts from China referring to "The Way," this is a translation of the word *tao*.

Because of this it's often said that Chinese Buddhism has been influenced by Taoism. To some extent that's true. But it's taking things too far when people insist that Chinese Zen Buddhism is actually a mixture of Buddhism and Taoism. Most of the ancient Buddhist masters of China were well aware that the terminology they were using was derived partially from Taoism, but they did their best with the language they had to make the proper distinctions. Which is not to say that these distinctions always got communicated to the less-educated populace.

I think it's important for Western Buddhists to make this kind of distinction between Buddhism and our own more established religions as well. But our culture values religious pluralism. We know too well the kinds of horrible things that can happen when one religion decides it's better than another and tries to wipe that other religion out. We're very sensitive to this. But I think sometimes we're too sensitive.

If I didn't believe that Zen was substantially better than anything else out there, I wouldn't bother with it. Why would I dedicate so much time and effort to something I believed was only just as good as anything else I could have gotten into? I don't think there's anything so terrible about saying this. I do not leap from my commitment to Zen to insisting that every other religion or philosophy should be destroyed. I know that other people find a lot of good in the paths they follow. Maybe those paths are better for them than Zen would be. I can't say. But I have no desire to force anyone else to see things the way I do. There's no point in that.

I've often told people that they can practice Zen and still hold on to their Christian beliefs, or for that matter any other religious beliefs they may hold. Since Zen is not a matter of belief it's not inconsistent to believe in whatever religion you wish. I usually warn them that their beliefs may start to change as a result of the practice, though. But you can be Christian with a Zen attitude. Or Jewish, Muslim, Rosicrucian, or whatever else with a Zen attitude. That's fine. I once met a woman at Tassajara who was fasting for Ramadan. It can be done! What concerns me more here is when people start hearing Zen stuff without the understanding that it's coming from a perspective very different from where religions come from.

When Buddhism gets mixed up with Christianity it's often subtle. Christianity is an idealistic religion. By this I mean that it proceeds from the belief that the immaterial, or spiritual, side of human experience is worthier than the material side. It values belief because belief is something that occurs within the mind or soul and the things that occur within the mind or soul are considered paramount.

I've seen this attitude transferred onto Buddhism many times. Buddhists in the West often become just as dogmatic about their beliefs as anyone else. I've personally been criticized rather viciously for not believing in what some Buddhists deem to be the correct things. I told you about what those guys over at e-sangha had to say about me. I'd like to dig into that a little further here.

What I was being taken to task for when they criticized me for not accepting the literal truth of rebirth was *believing the wrong things*. Because I hold the "wrong" beliefs, these folks said, I am not teaching Buddhism.

This is an excellent example of the contemporary Christian attitude toward belief being grafted onto Zen and expressed in language derived from Buddhism. The folks who ran e-sangha thought that one must adhere to a specific set of beliefs and express those beliefs in a particular way through accepted language in order to be considered a real Buddhist.

It's not just a Christian dogma that's been grafted onto Buddhism here, but a specific contemporary reading of Christianity that says the words of the Bible must be taken as literal truth. The folks on e-sangha were saying that the doctrines of Buddhism must also be taken literally. Anyone who doesn't believe that we literally get reborn in another form after we die, these guys think, is spreading dangerous heresy.

The funniest part of this is that I've said many times that I simply do not know what happens after we die. The fact is, I'd like to believe in literal rebirth just as much as they'd like to believe in it. Who wouldn't? Unfortunately, I find the belief a bit dubious. But I've already told you what I think of that.

The way e-sangha went after me clearly demonstrates the way the popular contemporary manner of understanding the Bible has been grafted onto Buddhism when there really is no precedent in Buddhism for doing so. I know of no ancient Buddhist masters who insisted that we had to take the things they said *literally* in the sense that the word *literally* has come to mean these days for lots of evangelical Christians. In fact, it's debatable whether even the authors of the Bible intended their stories to be taken literally in the sense that's come to mean these days.

One of the main reasons I got into Buddhism in the first place was that it did not insist that I had to take its literature literally. The ancient Buddhist masters understood that what constitutes taking something literally for one person might be entirely different for the person sitting next to her. Just because two people profess that they both believe Jesus Christ is the Son of God doesn't mean that they actually believe the same thing. They may, for example, have completely different notions about what it means to be the Son of God. Or they may regard Jesus Christ in absolutely incompatible ways. The more you dig into questions of belief, the more you see the impossibility of any two human beings ever really believing exactly the same thing.

The Mexicans I told you about hid their native god inside the Virgin Mary the same way so many of us hide the standard Western understanding of Christ inside our concept of Buddha. And we need to be keenly aware of this phenomenon.

A related problem is the mixture of Buddhism and other seemingly unconnected aspects of the cultures from which a lot of our Buddhist teachers come. A lot of people ask me about how we can separate what is truly Buddhist from the various cultural imports that often accompany Buddhism. Since I come from a Japanese Buddhist tradition, these folks often want to know how we can separate what is actually Buddhist from what is merely Japanese.

My own relationship with this problem is complicated. I lived in Japan for more than a decade. Because of this, the various items one finds in Buddhist temples don't immediately strike me as exotic the way they do most Americans. The altars look to me like fancier versions of the tables I often saw in people's houses. I can read some of the calligraphy hung on the walls, so it doesn't look to me like strange otherworldly squiggles. The tatami mats on the floor of the zendo look and feel like the tatami mats I had on the floor of my bedroom. When I enter a Zen temple I'm not instantly struck by the foreignness of it all the way lots of Westerners are.

I once did a lecture in Minneapolis at a place called Dharma Field.

Steve Hagen, the man who founded Dharma Field, was a student of Dainin Katagiri, that friend of Shunryu Suzuki I told you about earlier. Steve is very sensitive to the problem of sticking only to what is truly Buddhist and avoiding that which is merely Japanese. Dharma Field has no Japanese-style decorations. There's not even a Buddha statue on the altar. Instead, they have placed there a large rock that represents Buddha.

That's one good way to solve the problem. Another way to solve it is to accept that you can never really separate what is purely Buddhist from what is just Japanese. I don't really think that's what Steve is trying to do, anyway. In any case, much of what we take to be Japanese in Japanese Buddhism is actually adapted from things the Japanese Buddhists found in China. These Chinese items were, in turn, based on what Chinese Buddhists had seen in India. The things Indian Buddhists used were just adaptations of the common items they used for other purposes. Some of them were adopted from different cultures as well.

Rather than being overly concerned with separating the Japanese cultural elements from the core of "real" Buddhism, I think we have to be more careful not to dress up Christian dogma in Buddhist garments, so to speak. But we also have to accept that we're going to do a certain amount of that, no matter how hard we try not to. There may even be some aspects of Christian belief or of the general Western attitude toward things that Buddhism could benefit from. Nishijima Roshi used to say that he thought Americans were better equipped to understand Buddhism than Japanese people because he felt that American culture was much more pragmatic. So there may be many areas where a bit of mixing actually helps. I just think we have to watch it.

When we approach a nontheistic philosophy from a background steeped in monotheistic religion, we need to be aware of a lot of pitfalls. Let's look at some of those next.

CHAPTER 18

GOD HOLDS HIS OWN HAND

Western religion is monotheistic. The monotheism pioneered by Judaism was subsequently picked up by Christians and Muslims. Instead of a variety of gods who fulfill an assortment of roles, as in Hinduism, say, you just have one God who does it all. Sort of like a Walmart.

In Buddha's time Indian religion — what we call Hinduism these days, although it's arguably not a single religion but a group of related faiths — was polytheistic, and so it remains today. These days, though, many, if not most, Indians are familiar with the concept of monotheism, which they've heard from Christian missionaries as well as from Muslim conquerors. In Buddha's time the very idea was unknown. Nor was monotheism known in ancient China, Korea, or Japan. So the ancient Buddhist writers never had to deal with monotheism the way contemporary Buddhist writers do.

It may be that the ancient Indians were approaching something like monotheism for a few hundred years before Buddha appeared. You could say that the writers of the Upanishads were developing the concept of Brahman* into something like the monotheistic idea of God.

---

* The ultimate reality for Hindus.

And yet the belief in Brahman was not quite the same as the belief in Jehovah. Whereas the ancient Jews found it necessary to do away with all other gods completely — "Thou shalt have no other gods before Me," says the first commandment — the Indians left the other gods in place even as they developed the notion of an overarching sort of godhead figure called Brahman.

One of the things that excites a lot of Westerners when they encounter Eastern religions of various kinds, including Buddhism, is the idea that everything in the universe is really one. The idea that all things are a manifestation of a single underlying truth is about as close as you can get to monotheism in Buddhism.

My first Zen teacher's teacher was a guy named Kobun Chino. Kobun was an interesting character with a very personal take on Zen. He was kind of a Zen wild man in many ways. His style of teaching was deeply unconventional. Once he arrived so late for a lecture that the podium had been taken down and most of the audience had already left. He just stepped up front and said, "Thank you very much." Kobun was also unconventional in that he often talked about God. But his idea of God was pretty far removed from what most Westerners think of as God. He also had a unique take on the idea of all things being one. Kobun once said,

Wanting to be alone is impossible. When you become really alone you notice you are not alone. You flip into the other side of nothing, where you discover everybody is waiting for you. Before that, you are living together like that — day, sun, moon, stars, and food — everything is helping you, but you are all blocked off, a closed system.

It is very important to experience the complete negation of yourself, which brings you to the other side of nothing. People experience that in many ways. You go to the other side of nothing, and you are held by the hand of the absolute.

This piece reminds me of a phrase that Dogen uses in *Shobogenzo*. In Japanese it's *yui butsu yo butsu*. Sometimes this is translated as "only a Buddha and a Buddha." But I don't like that translation. It makes it sound as if two Buddhas could meet and discuss stuff. Which is true. But I don't think that's what Dogen was indicating. Nishijima Roshi translates it as "Buddhas alone together with Buddhas." This translation introduces the linguistic absurdity I think Dogen was getting at. The Buddhas in question are at the same time completely solitary and also interacting with each other.

Or we could say that God is alone and one, and he interacts with God. In Kobun Chino's words, "You are held by the hand of the absolute"; that is, God holds his own hand.

I especially like this quote because it brings up an aspect of God that often goes unmentioned by us Zen folk, and that aspect is love. In Christianity the idea of God's love is fundamental. "God so loved the world, that he gave his only begotten Son, that whosoever believeth in him should not perish, but have everlasting life," as it says in John 3:16, a quotation beloved by clown wig–wearing football fans all across America.

In a book called *Unsui: A Diary of Zen Monastic Life* a Zen monk named Giei Sato provides pictures he originally drew for children to explain to them what life in the monastery was like. To illustrate his experience of enlightenment he drew himself smiling gleefully with arms upraised standing in a gigantic hand representing the hand of Buddha. It beautifully expresses the feeling of absolute freedom within the warm embrace of the love of the universe that such an experience brings. Yet such images of love and warmth are rarely encountered in Zen. This isn't because there is no love and warmth in Zen, but because we tend to try and avoid the entanglements of emotionalism and sentimentality. These just get in the way of practice and are very different from true warmth and genuine love.

Because of this attitude some people misunderstand Zen and see it as icy and unfriendly. That's understandable because Zen has no tradition of proselytizing. Since Zen people don't feel any need to draw people into their religion, if indeed it even is a religion, we tend to be pretty blasé toward folks who express an interest, whereas other religions are usually extremely welcoming and encouraging. This makes us seem kind of aloof and frosty by comparison, when more often than not we're just being pragmatic.

Kobun was a bit different. His approach was generally warmer and more overtly openhearted than is the norm in Zen circles. Even so, once you get past the tough-seeming exterior, you'll find most of the people you meet in the Zen world care very deeply about everyone they meet. They just tend to be a bit more reserved in their expression of this caring.

Kobun also had this to say:

Wisdom doesn't come from anywhere; it is always there as the exact contents of awakening. What you can do is to uncover it, like going to the origin of a river. Have you been to the source of a river? It is a very mystic place. You get dizzy when you stay for a while. An especially big river has several sources, and the real source, the farthest point which turns to the major stream, is moist and misty, with some kind of ancient smell, and you feel cold.

From this place, the ancient call appears, "Why don't you know me? Living so many years with me, why can't you call my real name?" Unfortunately, we cannot travel into such place with this body and mind, but we feel there is such an origin, and from there everything starts. From that place you have come, actually, and whatever you do is returning to that spot.

In that *Shobogenzo* chapter I mentioned earlier about Buddhas alone together with Buddhas, Dogen quotes an ancient master who said, "Mountains, rivers, the earth, and human beings, are born together. The buddhas of the three times and human beings have always practiced together." He explains this by saying, "Thus, if we look at the mountains, rivers, and earth while one human being is being born, we do not see this human being now appearing through isolated superimposition upon mountains, rivers, and earth that existed before [this human being] was born."

Most of us conceive of ourselves as having been newly born into a preexisting world. We think that we are an isolated being who appeared at a certain time and at a certain time later will cease to be, or will go to heaven, or be reincarnated, or whatever.

But we ought to know better. Nothing in the universe can be created or destroyed. Everything that exists now has existed since the beginning of time, or perhaps even before that. It's changed forms, certainly. But it's always been here and can never go away. You could get overexcited about this and say it's reincarnation. But is it reincarnation when the heavy metals ejected from an exploding star coalesce over billions of years into the humans living on a planet light-years away? Perhaps it is in some sense. But it's easier to fantasize that you were Napoleon in a past life than to think about that exploding star being a manifestation of life just like you are. In any case, there's nowhere outside the universe for anything in the universe to go.

Dogen says, "Who is the person that has clarified, by investigating this birth from the side of this human being [who has been] born? Just what is, from beginning to end, this thing called 'birth'? We do not know the end or the beginning, but we have been born. Neither, indeed, do we know the limits of mountains, rivers, and the earth, but we see them here. Do not complain that mountains, rivers, and the earth are not comparable with birth. Illuminate mountains, rivers, and the earth as they have been described, as utterly the same as our being born."

So to understand what we really are, what God really is, we need only to open our eyes and our minds and allow ourselves and God to be as they are. The understanding we achieve may not be something we can easily communicate in words. But as Dogen says, we need not complain about this. Sometimes, though, we come across someone else who sees things the way we do. That's when the whole idea of oneness as it's usually understood gets turned on its head. Oneness is the truth. But you need someone else to see it with you.

This is what Dogen means when he refers to Buddhas alone together with Buddhas. We are all Buddhas. It's just that most of us don't know it, at least not yet. Not realizing what we really are is called delusion.

But Dogen says, "Delusion, remember, is something that does not exist. Realization, remember, is something that does not exist."

And God, said Eriugena, does not exist, either. Both Dogen and Eriugena are pointing to the same idea here. Realization — a Buddhist way of saying "God" — can't be said to exist because it's beyond existence and nonexistence.

Monotheism was a great innovation. It provided a way to understand how the universe worked. But it was still incomplete. And it had the unfortunate side effect of making people think that their monotheistic concept of God was better than other people's monotheistic concept of God. I spent some time last year in a place where people who believe in the very same God want to blow each other up because their concepts of that God differ in extremely minor ways. And it wasn't Jerusalem. Nope. These guys worshipped exactly the same God and even consulted the very same Holy Book to find out what God said. I want to talk a little about that next.

CHAPTER 19

NORTHERN IRELAND AND THE BUDDHIST CONCEPT OF GOD

The week before I went to Israel and met Lance Wolf, whom I wrote about way back in chapter 1, I was in Belfast, Northern Ireland. So in two weeks I got to see two different cultures divided by four different religions. All these religions are, ironically enough, incredibly alike. While Orthodox Muslims are hard to tell apart from Orthodox Jews without a scorecard, Catholics and Protestants are even more alike. But maybe that's why they're so antagonistic toward each other. Or maybe it has nothing to do with religion at all.

The first thing I noticed about Belfast was all the murals. They're everywhere. Some are three stories tall. Most are crudely drawn by artists without much understanding of perspective or of how to draw human eyes. Almost all the subjects of these murals are cross-eyed. They mainly show guys in black ski masks holding guns and baring their teeth. Some have slogans like "You are now entering Loyalist heartland," a warning for Catholics to stay away. Others convey various events in the city's troubled history.

Many of the more violent and disturbing murals, I was told, have been painted over with more neutral images. My favorite of these was in an alleyway around the corner from the Black Mountain Zen Center, where I was leading a retreat. It depicted all of Ireland's rock-and-roll heroes. Of course Van Morrison dominates the scene. I also spotted

Phil Lynott from Thin Lizzy, Bob Geldof of the Boomtown Rats and Live Aid, guitar hero Rory Gallagher, and several members of U2. Most of the rest I couldn't recognize.

In several parts of the city you can see what they call "Peace Walls." These are high concrete walls topped with barbed wire that run between Protestant and Catholic neighborhoods. The idea of erecting these walls was to curb some of the violence in these adjacent neighborhoods by making it harder for each side to enter the other's territory. Some say it works, while others say it increases tension and animosity and encourages continued segregation between the religions. Arguably violence in the city has lessened since the walls were put up. But it's hard to know if there is any cause-and-effect relationship.

Graffiti is ubiquitous in Belfast. The metal shutters on the bagel shop below the Black Mountain Zen Center sport the slogan "Regeneration is social cleansing." When I saw this I immediately thought of Doctor Who. In this long-running British science fiction series the title character regenerates every time one actor tires of playing the role, thus explaining why the same character looks completely different in the subsequent season. Actually, though, the word *regeneration* in this context is much like what we call *gentrification* in the USA, the process by which the poor and undesirable are moved out of a particular area so that the wealthy and desirable can live there. This makes the cities more beautiful and safer, but I always wonder where the displaced people go. They have to go somewhere, don't they?

It was very difficult for me to get a handle on what was going on in Belfast. I was only in town for a week, after all. During my retreat a Loyalist parade came by. There were guys with British flags, drummers, fife players, guys in bowler hats. The parade was followed by a couple of heavily armored paddy wagons and police offers sporting submachine guns.

One of the people I met in Northern Ireland told me that the men marching in that parade were basically terrorists. The government found it was better to allow them to have their parades than to stop them. It was a way of diffusing a potentially far more violent situation. I never did see anyone obviously representing the famed Irish Republican Army. My friends from the Zen center said that the IRA is far subtler in their tactics than the Loyalists are.

The folks at the Zen center told me that even Buddhists in Northern Ireland must declare themselves to be either "Catholic Buddhists" or "Protestant Buddhists." This is because there are quota programs in place to try and rectify some of the injustices of the past in terms of job placement and such. It sounded a bit like affirmative action programs in the United States. The government doesn't want people to try and get around these quotas by changing their official religion. So if your parents or grandparents were Protestants, and you're now a Buddhist, you're a Protestant Buddhist as far as the government is concerned.

In terms of what we usually call religion, this is all incredibly silly. It has nothing to do with anyone's belief systems. And it certainly has nothing to do with God.

The concept of God held by Catholics and Protestants is, for all intents and purposes, the same. One could argue about the belief in the Holy Trinity, the nature of the Bible as God's revelation, the clergy as God's intermediaries, and so forth as being different in the two faiths. But this is not what people in Belfast are arguing about. They're arguing about territorial rights and historical claims. They're arguing about battles that have been over and done with for hundreds of years. About the only religious matter you'll hear discussed there is the authority of the pope. But even this has little to do with his role in religion and everything to do with his political power.

This leaves a lot of people in Northern Ireland with a very dim view of God. When people's religions are nothing more than a convenient place to hang their grievances about other matters, it's easy to reject God entirely. And many people have.

Zen can seem like a good place to turn to if you're interested in the deeper, more spiritual aspects of life but are fed up with God and mainstream religion. As I noted earlier, a lot of people come to Zen practice as a way of rejecting or escaping from God. The problem for a lot of them comes when they start seeing that God and religion are not entirely absent from Zen.

This sometimes comes as a shock to lapsed Catholics and Protestants, as well as those who have left other religions. I've seen people react with real anger when the subject of God comes up in Buddhist contexts. They've been promised a religion without a God, so how dare I bring God into it?

I gave a talk at Bookfinders, a tiny used bookstore near the University of Belfast. I was excited because I found several back issues of the *Beano* comic book there. I used to read *Beano* when I was a little kid in Nairobi. You couldn't get American comic books in Kenya in those days, so I read British ones. Unfortunately, the people of Great Britain don't seem to value their comic book culture very much. Whenever I went into a comics shop in England and Northern Ireland looking for the British comics I used to read, they only had American and Japanese comics. Boring! So I was really jazzed to be able to get hold of a stack of back issues of *Beano*.

Here's a question I was asked by one of my hosts when I spoke at Bookfinders: "There's something I always wonder when people use the word *spiritual*. It's a kind of promiscuous word. The general assumption, I think, for most people who come from a Christian background, is that you mean that there's a spirit. We have a spirit. God's a spirit. There's a spirit of kindness. All the spirits will be reunited. There's something in all that baggage. But what does the term really mean?"

This is an important issue as regards the Buddhist concept of God. Take a look around you right now. There are all sorts of separate objects in your midst. Maybe there's a desk or a chair or a window or a wino passed out on the other side of the subway car you're reading this book on. The reason you're able to recognize these as distinct entities is because your brain is up there in your head doing all kinds of complex activities to distinguish things from one another. It does this so that you can navigate your way through the world efficiently.

But we know from contemporary scientific studies that at some level all this separation breaks down. In the microscopic realm, for example, the distinction between that wino and the subway seat he's lying on becomes hazy. Both wino and seat are made of essentially the same stuff. In Buddhist terms they are both manifestations of a single unified underlying reality that some might be so bold as to call God. But we won't go there just yet.

As I've already said I think that the most basic distinction the brain makes is between matter and the immaterial, or between matter and spirit. We need to make this distinction because we have to be able to discern the crucial difference between real objects out there in the world and the things we imagine or think about.

As I said, I suspect that it is impossible for the conscious part of the human brain to cross this barrier. It may be hardwired not to be able to do so. The consequences of not being able to differentiate between what's real and what's not are dire. Most of us have encountered people for whom that distinction has broken down. Sometimes it breaks down temporarily due to the use of drugs, especially psychedelics. Sometimes the breakdown is permanent, due to the effects of brain diseases. In any case, it's almost impossible to deal with someone who cannot distinguish between what is real and what he imagines to be real.

Part of the meditative path, though, is to gradually allow ourselves to become familiar with the fact that form and emptiness are actually the same thing. This has to be done very slowly, or the results can be catastrophic.

If we were to find ourselves crossing this barrier before we were ready to understand the full implications of what this means, we would be in even worse trouble than if we didn't cross it at all. This is one of the reasons I've waged a constant battle throughout my career as a writer and a monk against people who sell the public various schemes intended to get them enlightened quickly. What happens when you see the truth before you're ready for it is not enlightenment. It's what is commonly called psychosis.

Lots of psychotic people believe they understand layers of reality deeper than those accessible to ordinary people. And I think that in some cases they may be correct. But they've encountered these deeper levels of reality before acquiring the balance necessary to be able to navigate their way through the agreed-upon illusions human beings share.

I've said it before, and I'll say it again, because it's very important. Most religions start from the premise that the spiritual side of reality is the truth, while matter is either an unreal illusion or at best of far less importance than spirit. Our true nature, they say, is our spiritual nature. We are spirits in the material world. God, then, is the ultimate spirit. The world of matter is negligible at best or even nonexistent. I think this is what most people mean when they use the word *spiritual*.

But the Buddhist view of things is that God is neither spirit nor matter. Spirit and matter are manifestations of God. But God is neither one nor the other. He cannot be limited in that way.

The idea that things must be one way or the other is at the heart of conflicts like those in Northern Ireland and Israel. The brain is wired to accept only one solution to any problem and to reject all others. This system is usually efficient. But sometimes it breaks down. It's okay to say that there is only one truth. There is one real truth about the universe in spite of all our opinions about it. I think most of us agree with that. But that one truth can manifest in as many different ways as there are people to manifest that one truth.

If I had the solution to the problems of Belfast and Jerusalem I'd be a rich man. But I feel the solution lies within the ability to intuitively accept the reality of contradiction even in the face of our cognitive inability to do so.

This, of course, is easier said than done. Even saying it at all leaves most people completely confused. But things in the real world are never really one way or another. It's only our brains that force us to see them like that. It's our brain's job to do this. But luckily our brains are also able to accept things they don't really understand. This might be the true meaning of faith.

Faith in the sense I'm using it here does not mean accepting received truth merely because it has come from an authoritative source. It means having the faith to accept that you do not know certain things, that is, the ability to accept that you cannot possibly conceive of some things that are nonetheless true and important.

Maybe the solution to our problems with one another lies with this kind of faith in the unknown and unknowable. If we can all agree that none of us really knows what God actually is, maybe we can stop fighting about what we imagine God to be.

CHAPTER 20

HOTLINE TO HEAVEN

Before I went to Northern Ireland and Israel, I spent two weeks in Poland promoting the Polish edition of *Hardcore Zen*. My first audience there consisted of six people. I did a talk at a bookstore a few days later at which five people showed up, two of them employees of the bookstore. I led a meditation session and talk in another town, where three people showed up. I was not a major sensation in Poland.

Actually, not all my talks there did so poorly. The three-day retreat I led in Warsaw was well attended. I did a talk at a bar there that attracted a large and boisterous audience. And I spoke to a full house at a new age bookstore in Kraków with some really interesting folks in the çrowd.

It was raining when I landed at Kraków Airport. Poland was experiencing some of the worst nationwide flooding in decades. I was met at the airport by two representatives from my Polish publishers, Adam and Katarzyna, who thankfully also goes by Kaja, pronounced "ka-ya."*

Kaja was to be my Brad-sitter. Slawek, the president of the publishing company, had assigned her to mind me while I was in Poland. After

---

* I always make an effort to pronounce people's actual names right because I remember how happy I was in Japan when someone made an effort to pronounce my name correctly instead of calling me Buraddo. But I usually called Katarzyna Kaja.

a quick meal at a local vegetarian restaurant, Kaja took me to the train station and we soon settled in for a five-hour ride to Wrocław (mysteriously pronounced "vrotz-lov"), where I would be staying.

The train car we rode in looked like something out of a movie about the communist era. It was old and creaky, and the heater didn't quite work. There was a toilet at each end of the car. The light in one was burned out, and the other had someone's vomit all over the floor. I opted to use the one with the burned-out light. This was fine until sundown, after which I had to take careful aim and then shut the door and hope for the best in the dark.

Most of my talks in Poland were done through an interpreter — usually Kaja. She would do her best to try and convey what I was saying to the audience and then to convey the questions the audience asked back to me. You never know how much is getting through in situations like these. But I did my best.

I got a few odd, seemingly random questions. That new age bookstore I mentioned before was called Nalanda and it was in Wrocław. Someone there wanted to know about predictions he'd read about the future Buddha. I wasn't sure why he was asking me. Maybe he figured all Buddhists were concerned about such stuff.

The future Buddha thing is a little like the Second Coming of Christ in Christianity. When Gautama Buddha was alive he allegedly predicted that his teaching would last a few hundred years before falling into decline. After a long period of degeneration during which the dharma would be completely forgotten, he said, another Buddha would appear and set things straight. The name of this Buddha would be Maitreya. He never said exactly when Maitreya will appear. But it's supposed to be at a time when the oceans have shrunk in size and when people live to be eighty thousand years old. Obviously not quite yet.

Even so, a lot of people have already claimed that they are Maitreya. The thirteenth-century Japanese Buddhist monk Nichiren, a contemporary of Dogen, is believed by his followers to be Maitreya. In the twentieth century the philosopher Jiddu Krishnamurti was put forward by the Theosophical Society as Maitreya, though Krishnamurti himself never claimed to be him. L. Ron Hubbard, the founder of Scientology, said that he was Maitreya. There's a guy running around these days who calls himself Dorje Chang Buddha III (yes, that's Buddha the Third) who says he's Maitreya. And there's even a mixed martial arts guy from San Diego who says he's Maitreya. There are about as many people who believe they're Maitreya as there are who believe they're Jesus Christ. Maybe they should get together and have a convention.

I imagine the Polish guy who asked me this question has seen the claims of one or more of these people and wondered if they could be true. But to me, looking for the next Buddha is a little like looking for the next Beatles. In the seventies, rock magazines were always speculating on who was going to be the next Beatles, as if it was a given that a phenomenon like Beatlemania would happen again. Some people thought KISS was going to be it. Others thought Bruce Springsteen. The Ramones probably hoped it would be them. And it should have been. But it wasn't.

That's because there can never be a "next Beatles." The Beatles were a phenomenon that was intimately bound up with the times in which they appeared. Times change. Hitler was also a phenomenon of his times. And while there have been horrible racist dictators since Hitler, most notably Pol Pot in Cambodia, none of them ever had or ever could have had the kind of wide-ranging impact that Hitler did. Because Hitler wasn't just an individual; he was part of his times. His popularity had as much to do with the Treaty of Versailles and with the long history of anti-Semitism in Europe as it had to do with his personal charisma.

There can never be a next Buddha, either. All these people who claim to be the next Buddha are simply frauds. There will be no next Buddha and no Second Coming of Christ and no new Beatles. Look what happened when they tried to re-create the *Star Wars* phenomenon. So it's best to just drop the whole idea.

After Wrocław I traveled back south to Kraków to do a talk there.

By this time the rain was getting heavier. We were hearing alarming reports of rising river levels up north in Warsaw, which was our next destination. But still we pressed on. The place I stayed in Kraków reminded me of something out of *Monty Python and the Holy Grail*. The building appeared to have been constructed of damp stone about five hundred years ago, with electricity and plumbing added much later and not very efficiently at that.*

I didn't talk much about God in Poland. It seemed like a touchy subject. Catholicism is very strong there. During the communist era the government tried to suppress religion but failed. These days Pope John Paul II, the former Polish cardinal who served from 1978 until his death in 2005, is still highly revered. I was told that if you insult Jesus Christ in Poland, nobody gets too fussed. But if you insult Pope John Paul II, look out! There were Pope John Paul II souvenirs everywhere. It was clear that people just couldn't get enough of the guy.

The idea that God has a living representative on Earth — the pope — used to fascinate me as a kid. Since our friends the Kashangakis in Nairobi were Catholic I often wondered about the pope. Did he really know what God was thinking? Did he have a hotline to heaven? When I was a little kid, it seemed that things like that just might be possible.

I can't recall their answers. But an old Buddhist story relates to the pope and his ability to speak for God. It's about a Buddhist monk stuck in a tree. The monk is portrayed as hanging there with his teeth clenched tightly on a branch, with his hands and legs unable to get hold of anything. I can't imagine any way that could be physically possible. But that's the story. Just then a guy comes along and asks about Buddhism. If the monk opens his mouth to answer he'll fall and die. If he refuses to answer he will be neglecting his duty as a monk. When this koan is used in training the teacher often asks the student what the student would do in that situation.

I think this is sort of what the pope's dilemma is when speaking for

---

* It was probably nowhere near that old. But that's how it felt to me.

God. Some popes do a better job than others. But all of them are stuck with the same problem. They're no closer to God than anyone else. The less delusional of the popes seem to know this. And yet they have to say something.

Buddhist monks understand that the full truth of the universe, or the actual nature of God, cannot possibly be put into words. Yet people keep asking them to do so, and it's their duty to answer. Even if the monk has some understanding of the underlying basis of reality, he won't be able to convey that to someone who has not put in the work to try and come to terms with her true nature. It's a losing battle. Still, the monk has to say something.

I'm not sure how they work with this koan in the forms of Zen that use koans to teach. But I feel that the best answer would be the most honest expression of your own understanding at the moment the question is posed. You're going to lose your life anyway. It may be now. It may be decades from now. But at some point it's going to happen, and you have no idea when or how. So it's important to be true to yourself at every moment.

The rain kept getting fiercer and fiercer. When we drove north to Warsaw several major highways were washed out and we had to meander through a lot of back roads. This provided me with an interesting tour of the small towns of Poland but was very frustrating to my hosts, who were concerned about getting me to the places where I was supposed to speak on time.

Luckily, my final duty in Poland was to lead a three-day retreat in Warsaw at a center established by Philip Kapleau Roshi. So at least we wouldn't have to try and cross any flooded highways for a while. When we drove into town the word was that one of the major bridges was about to be swept away. A whole lot of people were standing on that bridge watching the rising river. I wondered what they planned to do if a wall of water suddenly came crashing toward them. They might not be able to get off in time to avoid being swept out to sea. Luckily for them that did not happen. But it got pretty close.

Out in the garden of the Zen Buddhist Centre of Warsaw the snails seemed happy about the rain. I saw a few pairs of gigundous snails mating. Snails have very sluggish — or is it snailish? — sex. I went out to the same spot each of the three days of the retreat and the same two snails were going at it for the entire time. At least there's some compensation for having to be born as a snail, I suppose.

Apparently while I was in Poland some Polish Zen chat room was all abuzz with questions of my legitimacy as a Zen teacher. I can't read Polish, but my hosts told me about it. I was being hosted by my publishers, who were understandably quite concerned about their reputation.

The problem those guys in Poland had seemed to center on whether I had completed the proper training course required for the title of Zen master, which, it seems, they took as a legitimate designation of rank. In Zen some teachers require their students to complete a certain curriculum of study before they designate them as teachers or so-called masters. Others are a whole lot looser about things. Nishijima Roshi, who ordained me, was one of the looser ones. He simply felt that I "got it" and that was enough. He knew I practiced daily, and I'd been with him for about seven years and with another teacher for about ten years before him. That was enough, as far as he was concerned.

I'm going to go off on a little bit of a tangent here, but this issue is important to me and I really want to get this down in print. I hope you'll bear with me. It does have a lot to do with God, I think. It's about how organizations try to claim God as their own. But this is nuts, because God cannot be owned.

These days a few organizations in the West would like to provide the kind of certification to Zen teachers that the Soto-shu, an organization that claims to officially represent Dogen's teachings, does in Japan. Like the Roman Catholic Church, such an organization would in effect take responsibility for the teachers it registers. That way you could know if the Zen master you met in, let's say, Dandelion Springs, Nebraska, was okayed by them by checking with the organization.

Such an organization could examine each registree's pedigree and make sure that she had completed the institution's curriculum and that she taught the institution's approved doctrines and practices. If a registered teacher got out of line, the organization would be able to force that teacher to mend his ways or they could excommunicate the teacher. The organization could also make it difficult for teachers with forged credentials to operate.

The problem with this is that such an organization would need to decide what it considers the minimum qualifications for a teacher. And there would be teachers who are perfectly legit whose dharma transmissions do not measure up to the standards of the organization — like me, for example, and like many of Kobun Chino's heirs, and a number of others in different lineages. These teachers would then be seen as less legit unless they went to the organization and did whatever the organization required of them.

This seems a lot like some of the things I used to do for Tsuburaya Productions, the company I worked for that made the superhero and monster movies. The monsters and superheroes we created were the intellectual property of the company. It was vital to the company's survival that we protect the image of these characters and made certain we earned money whenever someone used them. When someone used one of our characters without our permission or in some way we did not approve of, like putting them in porno films, which occasionally actually happened, we took legal action against them.

It's the same with organizations like the Roman Catholic Church and the Soto-shu. In a way, God is the intellectual property of the church — at least the church in question's specific definition of God. They deal with it in much the same manner as we dealt with Ultraman, our major superhero character. The church exercises control over who uses God and how he is presented, and they earn money from this usage. When someone uses God improperly the church doesn't sue, but they do often take action to stop or at least denounce that sort of usage.

But you can't really control God in this way. If you do, he's not God anymore. That kind of institutional control turns God into nothing more valuable than Mickey Mouse or Superman — or Ultraman. Mickey Mouse and Superman certainly do have some kind of value. But God is different. We need to allow people to create and define their own relationships with God. God is something different to each person who approaches him. When you try and standardize God, you end up with a dead God, stuffed and mounted, who might look beautiful but who can't do anything for anyone.

I don't have the solution to the problem of how to stop just anyone from calling herself a Zen master. But I do believe very strongly in lineage. Please understand, though, that this does not mean I think a person must have a Zen lineage in order to have something relevant to say. In fact, a lot of people outside the Zen world have plenty to say that puts most Zen teachers to shame.

But if you call yourself a Zen teacher, you'd better have some kind of lineage. Zen isn't about standardizing God. But by calling yourself a Zen teacher you are drawing on the collective history of Zen as a sort of authority. Or at least as advance advertising. It's like how you can choose to start your own perfectly delicious burger stand, or you can purchase a McDonald's franchise. If you go with Mickey D's you get the benefit of their name, their logo, the ads they take out on TV, and so on. If you start your own burger stand, you have to do all that stuff yourself. Your independent burger stand will probably be way better than any McDonald's.* But you'll have a much harder time making it in the business. This is precisely why there are fake Zen teachers.

Perhaps I'm wrong in feeling that a structured organization isn't the best solution to the problem of keeping those who claim to be Zen teachers honest. I certainly know I'm in the minority.

And I may be wrong about God as well.

---

* It could hardly be worse.

CHAPTER 21

WHAT GOD WANTS FROM YOU

I was checking my dreaded Twitter one day, and I saw that someone who calls himself Jinzang had tweeted the following: "Brad Warner is writing a book on why he thinks Buddhists believe in God. I say why he's wrong in my latest blog post."

In part his blog post says, "The most important thing to understand about emptiness is that it is a nonaffirming negative, which means that it denies that one thing is so without affirming that its opposite is so." This, the writer says, is "not just an intellectual quibble; it goes to the heart of what Mahayana Buddhist practice is all about." To prove his point he cites Edward Conze's translation of a sutra called *The Perfection of Wisdom in 8,000 Lines*, which says, "Even if perchance there could be anything more distinguished, of that too I would say it is like an illusion, like a dream. For not two different things are illusion and Nirvana, are dreams and Nirvana."

I could pull out a hundred quotes that prove Buddhism doesn't accept the existence of God if I were so inclined. I have already cited several in this very book. And the quotations I've used to try and show what I think is the Buddhist idea of God are all arguable. Besides, I can't make heads or tails out of the quotation he used!*

_____

* Sorry, Jinzang. You're a smart guy. But I really don't get this one!

If I haven't made the point enough already, let me say it again. Buddhism is not a religion based on a book. All literature, including Buddhist literature, is written by people who have their own reasons for saying the things they say. Besides that, Buddhism has a lot more literature than any other religion I know of. Even if it *were* based on books, it would not be based on a single book like the Bible, the Qur'an, or the Torah. It's got hundreds of sutras that are considered more or less canonical and are accepted by the majority of Buddhists as authentic.

Even if we were to narrow it down to the Pali Canon, which supposedly preserves the words and deeds of the historical Buddha, there is still a huge amount of material. Within such a vast library you can find quotations to support just about any position you like. This is also true of the shorter scriptures of other religions. But the problem becomes magnified by a couple hundredfold when it comes to Buddhism.

As you know, I have problems with words like *emptiness* and *nirvana* and *Buddha nature* and all the rest of them as they seem to be understood by contemporary Western Buddhists. These words are often taken by Western readers as things that happen in our heads. Even approaching a phrase like *nonaffirming negative* requires one to do some mental gymnastics just to get a grip on what's being talked about.

The word *God*, on the other hand, is much more immediate and richer. Rather than asking you to ponder its meaning, the word *God* just punches you in the face, after which you have to deal with how to respond. It has all kinds of messy layers of meaning and connotation. It sparks emotions and tangents. Sometimes it makes people feel settled and happy. Sometimes it makes them angry. Or it makes them confused. Or it makes them frustrated. Or all of the above at the same time. It's a dangerous word.

That's what I've encountered in my practice. Zen is not something dry and orderly. It cannot be easily fit into premeasured boxes. It's very messy, because it is alive. The universe we inhabit is a dynamic, living thing. *God* is a good word to use for what Zen is about because shoving the word *God* into a tidy intellectual container would be like trying to shove a live octopus into a Kleenex box.

When we try and run away from this messiness into the sphere of rigorously reasoned thought or into vague words that have no real meaning to us, we're losing something literally vital. This is not a trivial matter.

My Twitter friend is not the only one on the Interwebs upset by my insistence on using the word *God* in the context of Buddhism. An anonymous commenter on my blog said, "In our day, here in the US for example, eternalism/dualism is enshrined by the word *God*. You have to really pretend the word means something it does not mean to get away from that fact."

In fact, I don't feel I have to pretend it means something it doesn't. The fact that eternalism/dualisim is enshrined by the word *God* is one of the many facets of it that makes the word so useful, I think. The nature of my practice has always been that whenever I believe I've finally figured out what things mean, there's always another aspect that I've missed. Just when I believed Buddhism was all about getting rid of eternalism and dualism, there it was in the very fabric of the universe itself, something eternal and dualistic.

Another blog commenter who identifies himself as the Rev. Uncle Willie wrote, "It seems to me that 'gods' are simply masks, usually anthropomorphic, that people hang on the universe, or parts of the universe, because they find it difficult or impossible to relate to a complex and impersonal universe. The 'god' mask is an illusion and the universe is the reality behind the illusion. All other explanations seem to be just rationalizations for irrational beliefs."

And yet my experience of the universe is that it is not impersonal at all. I told you how my first Zen teacher said, "It's more you than you could ever be." That is precisely my impression as well. The universe, which I had thought to be vast, complex, and utterly impersonal, was, in fact, also intimate, simple, and intensely personal, even loving — while at the same time being vaster, more complex, and more impersonal than I could ever have imagined it to be. I know that sounds impossibly contradictory. But it's that too; it's contradictory in ways you wouldn't even suppose it could be contradictory.

That's just a small sampling of the objections made to this book you're reading before it was even published. Now that it's been unleashed onto the world, I expect the objections to become even stronger. This is not easy stuff. But then again, easy stuff doesn't interest me all that much.

I received another comment on my blog that I'd like to tell you about. This one wasn't quite so critical. It said, "I appreciate that you go out of your way to emphasize that you're a normal guy with doubts and feelings just like the rest of us, but in a lot of your posts you've also written about making an effort to understand 'what the universe wants you to do,' or things to that effect. I've been dealing with some self-doubt and anxiety lately and the promise of being able to know what the freakin' UNIVERSE wants for me sounds very appealing right now. How does that…um…work, exactly?"

In Luke 22:42, Jesus says, "Father, if thou be willing, remove this cup from me: nevertheless not my will, but thine, be done." He's in the Garden of Gethsemane, near where Lance Wolf was murdered two thousand years later, and he knows he's about to be betrayed and then taken away to be tortured and killed. It is not a pleasant prospect.

Mark, Matthew, and Luke, the first three Gospels in the New Testament, are known as the synoptic gospels. All the synoptic gospels contain a line in which Jesus accepts his terrible fate, even Mark, in which Jesus expresses the greatest doubts about his mission. All three books tend to agree on most key points, and they are regarded as the most likely to be historically accurate, though the degree to which they may be historically accurate is a topic of endless debate. In the synoptics Jesus is always a bit unsure during this scene. The Gospel of John, which is not one of the synoptic Gospels, was composed decades later, and in it Jesus is pretty much superhuman. He has no doubts there in the garden. He coolly says, "The cup which my Father hath given me, shall I not drink it?" just like an action hero. I don't think it went down like that at all.

We all have doubts and anxiety about what we ought to do with our lives. You do. I do. Contrary to what John says, I'm sure Jesus did too. Buddha did, and these doubts are often depicted in the sutras as the temptations of Mara, an evil Satan-like being. It would be nice to believe that there is a God somewhere out there, and if we could just ask him what we were supposed to do, he could give us an answer. Unfortunately, it doesn't work that way. I don't think there is a God like that at all, even though I do believe in God. The synoptic gospels seem to be teaching us this lesson, while the Gospel of John wants us to believe in a savior who could be played by Bruce Willis or Chuck Norris.

But action heroes have scripts to work from. The outcome for them is already set. Some guy with a laptop in a Starbucks in the Hollywood Hills is going to make more money for typing up a few lines about his made-up hero's escape from the bad guys than you or I will ever see in our lifetimes. All the hero has to do is say those lines, and he's golden.

Our lives aren't like that. The outcome is not already figured out for us. In this moment we have an infinite number of choices and an infinite number of possible outcomes. Our past is already set, and our future becomes determined the moment we choose to act, though each action we take determines a new future.

I am a terribly indecisive person. This is one of my great failings. If not for my years of Zen practice I am certain I would have been paralyzed by indecision at every turn. As it is, it's all I can do sometimes to overcome it. I have to take a leap of faith and make a move.

Even the simplest decisions can cause me anxiety. I'm a big music collector, but nobody should ever accompany me to a record store because I will spend hours agonizing over whether or not to buy a particular CD. And that is an easy decision. When it comes to more important things, I'm a total mess.* And yet I believe that I intuitively know at every moment exactly what I ought to do next, even when it comes to whether I ought to buy yet another remastered version of The Who's *Quadrophenia*. It's just that I also think way too much and thereby muddy the waters.

In Zen we talk in terms of taking aim rather than achieving specific goals. You aim at the goal and let your arrow fly. Depending on your skills and luck your arrow might hit the target, or it might not. Even if you're the most skillful archer in the world, a sudden gust of wind could come along and redirect your arrow miles from the target. That's why even the best archers in the world can't guarantee that they'll always hit every target.

Knowing what the universe wants doesn't imply that the universe manifests itself as a burning bush and says to you, "Lo and verily, Ichabod, you should ask Belinda to the prom and not Mandy. Even though Mandy is way hotter now, she's going to be a drug addict when she gets to be twenty-three, and you'll be stuck with her, whereas Belinda is really fantastic in ways I'm not even going to tell you."

It just doesn't work like that. And, believe me, I really wish it did.

In terms of rules, I already talked about the ten Buddhist precepts that one is recommended to follow if one wants to live a happy life. Because they're so important, I'm gonna list them again here. They are 1) Not to kill, 2) Not to steal, 3) Not to misuse sexuality, 4) Not to lie, 5) Not to cloud the mind with intoxicants, 6) Not to criticize others, 7) Not to be proud of oneself and slander others, 8) Not to covet, 9) Not to give way to anger, and 10) Not to slander Buddha, Buddhist teachings, or the Buddhist community.

These aren't rules you need to obey lest you face punishment from God — at least not in the usual sense. God is the universe. So you can

---

* Well, maybe not a *total* mess. I wouldn't be doing what I'm doing now if my own assessment of myself were completely true. But I'm trying to make a point here.

expect some kind of adverse reaction if you choose to go against what the universe wants. But there is no judge who sits on high and decides whether or not you have obeyed the law. Rather, the law of cause and effect works in the same way that grabbing a burning bush to make it stop talking to you causes your hand to get burnt. And God is also you. So it's you dealing with yourself for what you know you did wrong.

The precepts seek to address the most common situations a person might face and provide the most common solutions to moral conundrums. Thus, if your intuition fails, your best bet is to follow the precepts. On the other hand, there may be rare times when breaking the precepts, at least as they are written, might actually be the more moral choice.

For example, killing a maniac who was running around the neighborhood with a gun shooting random people would be the best way to uphold the precept of not killing. Stealing medicine necessary to save someone's life when neither you nor that person can afford to pay would be the best way to avoid breaking the precept of not stealing. But these are very unusual circumstances. Most of us won't ever encounter them.

So it's important to follow the precepts. But it's also important to know when to be flexible about what they mean. In Buddhism there is a rather weird idea that we always know what the precepts really mean. Sam Harris hints about that a little in his book *The Moral Landscape*. It's not that morals are arbitrary or defined by society. Rather, we all have within us a sense of what is actually moral.

All of us are expressions of the universe. Dogen talked about that when he said that we're the eyes and ears *it* uses to experience the world. We are not merely confused little robots wheeling around on the stage of life. We are manifestations of life itself.

Nishijima used to say in his talks on Saturday afternoons at the Young Buddhists Society at Tokyo University that Zen practice allows us to do exactly what we want. What the universe wants — what God wants — and what we actually want are precisely the same thing. The problem is that our big brains get in the way, much in the way that mine does when I'm trying to decide what CD to buy in a record store.

We use our brains to create a very believable facsimile of what we imagine ourselves to be. We can then manipulate that facsimile in our minds and predict the outcome of future events with a fair degree of accuracy, as long as the event in question is pretty straightforward. For example, we can imagine what would happen if we stepped onto the 405 Expressway in Los Angeles at the height of rush hour.* We can imagine what would happen if we opened a can of chocolate pudding and ate it all in one big gulp. But very often, even in these simple cases, our imagined outcome is not exactly what happens. We simply cannot account for all the variables, no matter how clever we are.

Yet we can still do tremendous things with this ability. We can work out the precise calculations needed to put a man on the moon and then make it actually happen, to take one clichéd but good example. Stuff like this makes us imagine that the predictive abilities of our thinking brain might be limitlessly powerful. It makes us imagine that we ought to be able to predict the outcome of any situation, and it makes us feel like losers if we fail to do so. At least I know that's how I sometimes feel. And I don't think I'm alone in this.

We also know from experience that we often get things completely wrong when we try and make predictions. We catalog the times we got things like this wrong into the box labeled "times I failed to predict an outcome correctly." And if you're me, you write under that "because I'm really stupid."

But it's not stupid at all. It's just normal.

Malcom Gladwell's book *Blink: The Power of Thinking without Thinking* goes into great detail about the mountains of scientific research that show how intuition works. It also talks about how we generally just

---

* Probably nothing because the cars come to a dead stop for most of the afternoon. But you get my point.

muck things up by deliberately thinking about them. It's an important book, and I'm glad to see that science is catching up with Buddhism. But the entire time I was reading the book, I kept thinking, "This is what my Zen teacher has been saying for years." It's what a lot of Zen teachers have been saying for years. In *Fukanzazengi* ("Recommending Zazen to All People") Dogen speaks of this, calling it "the wisdom that knows at a glance." That was eight hundred years ago.

So how can we know what the universe, or God, wants us to do? I know, I know, putting it in terms of God is very dangerous. For one thing, some of us imagine that God is a guy (or gal!) just like us. And, like us, he has his moods. What God wants one day might be completely different from what he wants the next.

But God isn't a guy just like us. He is, in fact, *us*. I know that loads of people get quite upset over the notion that we, ourselves, are God. This is because they have some very specific ideas of what God is, and obviously we are not like that.

So what do I mean when I make this absurd assertion?

I mean that the universe, that is, God, manifests in as many ways as it can. Infinite ways. Forever. We are all part of the whole of this infinity. We are each of us infinite. Not in some future afterlife — we are infinite right now. We as individuals are not the whole except in terms of the way we partake of the whole. We are limited. We live a while, and then we stop living. After that we do not return. These are contradictions. Life is full of them. Get used to it.

God, in my way of thinking, is not only omniscient and omnipresent. He is also just as stupid and limited as any of his manifestations. So while God knows exactly what he wants, he also doesn't know what he wants at all. That's precisely what makes him so omniscient. He even knows the feeling of deepest ignorance in all its possible manifestations.

My friend and first Zen teacher, Tim McCarthy, wrote a poem about God. Part of it goes like this:

God, she said over soup,
cannot add or subtract from who He is
You believe in God then?
He doesn't want me to
knowing, as He does,
that God does not exist.

All fingers grasp the edge
of this cliff. All other moments
are absent.

Tim often talks about how God knows that God doesn't exist. Which is sort of like saying that there is no God and he is always with you. God doesn't want us to believe in God because God knows there is no God. Yet I believe in God anyhow. Go figure! God is knowledge as well as ignorance. Our contemporary Judeo-Christian culture can't handle such a contradiction. But there is evidence this wasn't always so. According to Elaine Pagels, in her book *Revelations*, in Nag Hammadi, Egypt, a hymn called "Thunder, Perfect Mind" was discovered in which God says:

I am the honored one, I am the scorned one
I am the whore and the holy one...
I am the barren one, and many are her children.

Ambiguity is fundamental to the fabric of the universe. We are alive only because the universe insists that things be two ways at once. Or more than two. So in such a state of total ambiguity, how can we know what to do?

Nishijima Roshi's idea about doing exactly what you want has been really helpful to me. It's a good way to put it. Intuition is the universe telling you what you really want to do. The problem is that we have been taught since birth to drown out our intuition with thought before we can really even understand what those intuitions are.

The only way I know of to get in touch with what God wants is to be very, very, very quiet. This is not easy to do. You have been taught since birth to make your mind as noisy as possible. To sit down and shut up — in other words, to do Zen practice or at least something like it — takes a great deal of effort. But it's worth it.

So go ahead and do it, and see what God wants from you.

CHAPTER 22

GOD IS SILENCE

In the book of Kings, verses 11 and 12, it says, "And, behold, the Lord passed by, and a great and strong wind rent the mountains, and brake in pieces the rocks before the Lord; but the Lord was not in the wind: and after the wind an earthquake; but the Lord was not in the earthquake: And after the earthquake a fire; but the Lord was not in the fire: and after the fire a still small voice."

I would say that the author of the book of Kings didn't take it quite far enough. Maybe God doesn't have a "still small voice." Maybe he has no voice at all. Maybe God is silence.

And yet if you're quiet enough you can learn to listen to silence, to listen to nothing, and to learn from nothing.

Most of the ways that Western culture has developed for relating to God are much too loud. We make a joyful noise unto the Lord, as the book of Psalms enjoins us. But our noise is too darned noisy for us to hear the reply. We can't hear the silence that underlies all that noise.

Silence is contained in everything. And everything is contained in silence. When we are very quiet, we align ourselves with our own silence.

You don't need to find perfect quiet in order to be with silence. Perfect quiet is a myth. I've been in isolated mountain temples in Japan where the cicadas were almost deafening, and I've been in sensory-deprivation tanks in Canada where I could hear people walking around on the floor above me. Perfect quiet doesn't happen on this planet. But silence is everywhere. Even in the noise of contemporary life there is always silence.

Silence is here right now.

In the Dhammapada, Buddha says, "When one knows the solitude of silence, and feels the joy of quietness, one is then free from fear and sin and feels the joy of the dharma."

We've forgotten silence. We crave noise and stimulation. When we're not stimulated enough we feel unfulfilled, cheated. We get bored too easily, even with access to all sorts of excitement, literally right at our fingertips every second of every day. We've forgotten that all creativity arises from silence. And as Katagiri Roshi, the late head of the Minneapolis Zen Center, said, we need to return to silence.

Perhaps the ultimate creation arose from the silence of the void. Perhaps our whole universe is God's dreaming in the silence.

Tim McCarthy once said to me, "You share identity with all things and you are responsible for all things, and a natural love for all things just happens to be present and you recognize that." God is one, but God has infinite identities. God shares his identity with all of us, just as we share our identities with God.

When we were both in our early twenties, my friend Joe and I had a conversation I've always remembered. He stated that he didn't know if he could believe in God. I replied that I thought God was the most obvious thing and that I had trouble believing in everything else.

Reflecting on that conversation, I sometimes wonder what made me say that. At that age I hadn't had any real experience of God through zazen practice; I'd only just begun the practice a few years earlier. Yet I must have felt God's presence.*

I took a chance on meditation practice many years ago. I trusted Tim McCarthy. I had faith in him in the original sense the early Christians

---

* Or maybe I was just being contrary. Who knows?

meant by that word, meaning I felt trust and commitment. I trusted that he was not handing me a bunch of bullshit, and so I committed to the practice as a part of my everyday lifestyle. From the time I met Tim, at age nineteen, until now I have rarely gone a day without sitting still and staring at a blank wall. I am forever grateful to him for introducing me to this stupidly simple practice. It saved my life. It showed me God.

God is not the possession of any religion. If anything, religion can be a path away from God. God cannot be bound up inside churches, synagogues, mosques, and temples. Those are just community centers where people gather to hang out with their friends. God is no more to be found in those places than he is in rock clubs or back-alley bars. God is in the wilderness, and God is in the city. Everywhere you go God is there. God walks with you. God is you, and God is the very act of walking.

When Americans start talking nonsense about putting God back into our schools or insisting that our nation is more "under God" than any other, it makes me ill. That kind of God is just a warped fantasy. The kind of God that hates homosexuals or glories in violence is absurd. Thankfully, he'll be gone soon — maybe not soon enough. But he isn't going to be with us much longer. Thank God! It may not seem that way now. But when we look at the broad sweep of history, we see that the more fanatical believers in God have been losing ground for centuries. Sure, there may be a few in Congress now. But they used to run entire continents!

I've spent this whole book trying to say something about God. But in the end, you can't really say anything about God. Anything you say limits God and therefore is a mistake.*

But we need to acknowledge God's presence. Yes, when we try to possess God and freeze him in books and enshrine him in temples we go terribly wrong. And when we say that because the stuff in those books

---

* But please don't return this book to the shop because of that! There were a few jokes in here too!

isn't God and because our temples aren't the home of God then there is no God at all, we also go wrong.

When we forget God we make as big a mistake as we do when we insist that our concept of God is the only one that matters. When we forget God we treat one another and the world we live in as objects. We fail to recognize that whenever we harm someone else or the world we live in, we only harm ourselves.

Of course, some people don't like to use the word *God*, and that's perfectly understandable. The word *God* has been abused for centuries and continues to be abused. I'd like it if there was a better word, but so far I haven't found one. No other word is big enough or divisive enough to do the job. God is too huge to be called anything but God. And God demands too much of us to be called by any name that politely tiptoes around all the ugly morass of differing opinions about his nature.

People often ask me what I hope to accomplish in my books. I never know how to answer that question. I'm not sure what I want to accomplish. I'm not sure if the word *accomplish* is even relevant to what I set out to do with this or with any of my other books.

Our world is in trouble. It's been in trouble for a very long time. But now the threats to our survival are particularly urgent. We have unprecedented access to incredibly dangerous technology without the necessary grounding in reality to avoid doing the worst with them. We are still addicted to our own sense of self and our mistaken belief that we must defend that self at all costs. In Alcoholics Anonymous they say you need to have faith in a higher power to help you overcome your addictions. You can't do it alone, they say. I like that approach.

Perhaps if we have faith — trust and commitment, that is — in the universe we live in as God, we can work together to find the solutions we so desperately need. We aren't living things inhabiting a dead universe. The universe we live in is, just like us, an expression of life itself. Once we understand this, we will start taking better care of our world and of one another.

ABOUT THE AUTHOR

Brad Warner was born in Ohio in 1964. In 1983 he met Zen teacher Tim McCarthy and began his study of Zen while he was still the bass player of the hardcore punk band Zero Defex, whose big hit was the eighteen-second masterpiece "Drop the A-Bomb on Me!" In the 1980s he released five albums of psychedelic rock under the band name Dimentia 13 (that's the way he spelled it), though Dimentia 13 was often a one-man band with Brad playing all the instruments. In 1993 he moved to Japan, where he landed a job with Tsuburaya Productions, the company founded by Eiji Tsuburaya, the man who created Godzilla. The following year Brad met Gudo Nishijima Roshi, who ordained him as a Zen monk and made him his dharma heir in 2000. Brad lived in Japan for eleven years. He published his first book, *Hardcore Zen*, in 2003, followed by *Sit Down and Shut Up!* in 2007 and *Zen Wrapped in Karma Dipped in Chocolate* in 2009 and *Sex, Sin, and Zen* in 2011. These days he travels around the world leading retreats, giving lectures, and looking for cool record stores. At last report he was living in Los Angeles.

He can be found on the web at hardcorezen.info.

NEW WORLD LIBRARY is dedicated to publishing books and other media that inspire and challenge us to improve the quality of our lives and the world.

We are a socially and environmentally aware company, and we strive to embody the ideals presented in our publications. We recognize that we have an ethical responsibility to our customers, our staff members, and our planet.

We serve our customers by creating the finest publications possible on personal growth, creativity, spirituality, wellness, and other areas of emerging importance. We serve New World Library employees with generous benefits, significant profit sharing, and constant encouragement to pursue their most expansive dreams.

As a member of the Green Press Initiative, we print an increasing number of books with soy-based ink on 100 percent postconsumer-waste recycled paper. Also, we power our offices with solar energy and contribute to nonprofit organizations working to make the world a better place for us all.

Our products are available
in bookstores everywhere.
For our catalog, please contact:

New World Library
14 Pamaron Way
Novato, California 94949

Phone: 415-884-2100 or 800-972-6657
Catalog requests: Ext. 50
Orders: Ext. 52
Fax: 415-884-2199
Email: escort@newworldlibrary.com

To subscribe to our electronic newsletter, visit:
www.newworldlibrary.com

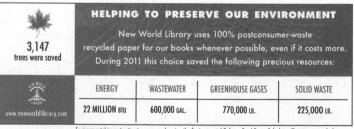

HELPING TO PRESERVE OUR ENVIRONMENT

3,147 trees were saved

New World Library uses 100% postconsumer-waste recycled paper for our books whenever possible, even if it costs more. During 2011 this choice saved the following precious resources:

ENERGY	WASTEWATER	GREENHOUSE GASES	SOLID WASTE
22 MILLION BTU	600,000 GAL.	770,000 LB.	225,000 LB.

www.newworldlibrary.com

Environmental impact estimates were made using the Environmental Defense Fund Paper Calculator @ www.papercalculator.org.